Annual Survey 2

UK Government & Politics

**Paul Fairclough, Richard Kelly
& Eric Magee**

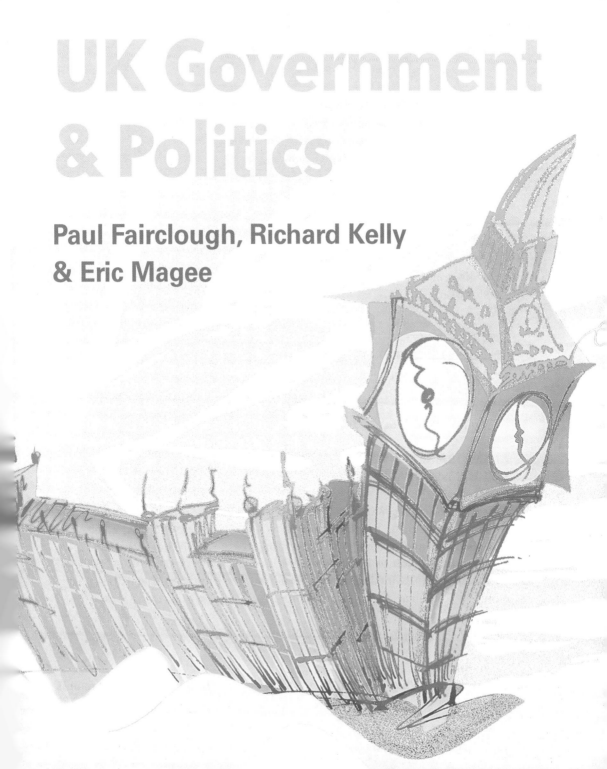

Philip Allan Updates
Market Place
Deddington
Oxfordshire
OX15 0SE

tel: 01869 338652
fax: 01869 337590
e-mail: sales@philipallan.co.uk
www.philipallan.co.uk

ISBN–10: 1-88489-423-1
ISBN–13: 978-1-84489-423-9

Printed by Raithby, Lawrence & Co Ltd, Leicester

Environmental information
The paper on which this title is printed is sourced from managed, sustainable forests.

Contents

Chapter 1

The 2005 general election: an indefensible electoral system?

About this chapter

The 2005 general election served to reignite debate about the Westminster electoral system. In this chapter, we will address the following key questions:

- Has the election strengthened the case for first-past-the-post (FPTP)?
- Has the election strengthened the case for electoral reform?
- How has the election affected party attitudes to electoral reform?
- Are there now too many different electoral systems in the UK?

FPTP vindicated?

For the supporters of FPTP, the key point in 2005 was that, once again, the electoral system prevented a hung parliament — even though no party achieved even 40% of votes cast. From this a number of other 'benefits' flowed:

- **The UK government was formed quickly**. Blair announced his new cabinet the day after the election. This asset was underlined 3 months later by events in Germany, when a general election under proportional representation (PR) produced stalemate and governmental paralysis.
- **The UK is governed by its most popular party**. Labour won 3% more votes than the Tories and 13% more votes than the Liberal Democrats.
- **The UK government does not give disproportionate influence to small parties**. Parties like the Liberal Democrats remain in opposition — the ideal place, it is argued, for those with less than a quarter of the votes cast.
- **The UK government looks stable**. There is no reason to expect another general election before 2009.

FPTP incriminated?

However, for critics of FPTP, the 2005 election also offered compelling reasons for change:

- **A clear majority of MPs (66%) were elected without majority support**. A classic example of how this happens, and how it distorts voters' wishes, is shown in Table 1.1. A majority of constituents in Belfast South voted for Protestant/unionist parties (the DUP and UUP). But because the unionist vote was split, the constituency now has a Catholic/nationalist MP.

Candidate	Share of the vote (%)
McDonnell (Social Democratic and Labour Party)	32
Spratt (Democratic Unionist Party)	28
McGimpsey (Ulster Unionist Party)	23

Table 1.1 Unwanted outcomes? The case of Belfast South, 2005

- **FPTP again produced a disproportionate House of Commons**. Labour won only 35% of votes but 55% of seats, while the Liberal Democrats won only 11% of seats in return for their 22% of votes (see Table 1.2). 'Disproportional representation' also affected the Tories — notably in England, where they won more votes than Labour (35.7% compared to 35.5%) but 93 fewer seats.

	Share of UK vote (%)	Seats won	Estimated seats won under PR
Labour	35	355	227
Conservatives	32	197	209
Liberal Democrats	22	62	142

Table 1.2 Disproportional representation, 2005

- **FPTP again produced a government unsupported by most voters**. The government won its majority of 65 with just 35.2% of votes cast in the UK — the lowest vote share ever recorded by a single-party government. With turnout again low (61.5%), the government was supported by just 21.6% of eligible voters — again, a record low for a governing party. It is worth noting that, when the Tories suffered one of their worst ever defeats in the 1997 election, they still polled more votes than Labour did in 2005. Moreover, Labour's vote share was lower than in 1979, when it lost, while its total vote was lower than in 1987 — when it lost by a landslide. Labour's failure to 'win England' is crucial for two reasons: England is where most UK voters live; and, following the devolution of power to Wales and Scotland, England's voters are those most affected by the decisions of the UK government.
- **FPTP was heavily biased towards the Labour Party**. Whereas Labour won a seat for every 26,895 votes polled, the Liberal Democrats won a seat for every 96,486 votes polled. When the Tories last won a general election, in 1992, they had 41% of votes, a 7% vote lead and a majority of just 21 seats. Labour in 2005 had 35% of votes, a 3% vote lead — and a majority of 65.
- **Labour needs less support than its main rivals to win seats**. First, due to a steady population drift from towns to suburbia, the average Labour seat now contains 6,000 fewer voters than the average Tory seat. Second, turnout is 7% lower in an average Labour seat than in an average Tory seat. Though pleasing for Labour, this does not augur well for FPTP. Electoral systems need cross-party support to survive — and only Labour now seems to have a vested interest in FPTP.

- **The safe seats produced by FPTP may have contributed to low turnout.** This looked especially likely in safe Labour seats, where average turnout was only 55%. In Liverpool Riverside, where Labour's 2001 majority was over 19,000, turnout was just 48%.
- **FPTP may obstruct diverse representation.** Although the 721 women candidates and 128 women MPs were record numbers, these figures still represent only a fifth of the total, while women make up over 50% of the adult population. Likewise, the three main parties fielded only 113 candidates from ethnic minorities, of whom only 15 were elected. With its single-member constituencies, FPTP only permits local parties to choose one candidate — and local parties may still 'play safe' when choosing.
- **FPTP threatens even worse outcomes.** According to John Curtice, the 2005 voting patterns indicate that: Labour could win a majority of seats with just 29% of votes cast; if the Tories have a vote lead of 1–4%, Labour could still win a majority of seats; and if the Tories have a poll lead of 4–10%, Labour will still have enough seats to cause a hung parliament — the very thing FPTP is supposed to avoid. This would give us all the problems of PR (such as shaky coalitions) without any of the benefits (the parties' share of seats would still be disproportionate to their votes). In such circumstances, FPTP would be virtually indefensible.
- **FPTP in 2005 compared badly with the recent performance of other UK electoral systems.** Fans of electoral reform say that FPTP looked even more disreputable in 2005 when compared to the record of other electoral systems used in the UK between 2003 and 2004. For example, the European elections of 2004, conducted under the party list system, recorded a high level of proportionality (Labour getting 24% of seats for 23% of votes), while providing some representation for parties like UKIP and the Greens — thus reflecting the diversity of the modern electorate. The Scottish Parliament and Welsh Assembly elections of 2003, conducted under the additional member system, used multi-member constituencies which seemed to abet gender equality (half the Welsh Assembly members and a third of the Scottish Parliament are now women). Finally, the mayoral elections of 2005 showed the various strengths of the supplementary vote (SV) system (see box below).

Supplementary vote in action, 2005

The SV system was used for the four mayoral elections in Doncaster, Hartlepool, Stoke-on-Trent and North Tyneside. Under SV, voters express a first and second preference vote. If no candidate has a majority of first preference votes, all but the two most popular candidates are eliminated. The second preference votes of those who supported the eliminated candidates are then examined: those that are cast for either of the two remaining candidates are then added to their total; whichever of those candidates then has the highest total is elected. The North Tyneside result, which is given in the table below, provides both a vindication and a criticism of SV as an example of 'majoritarian representation'.

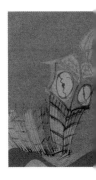

	1st preference votes	2nd preference votes	Total
Linda Arkley (Con)	35,457	3,991	39,458
John Harrison (Lab)	34,053	6,407	40,460
Joan Harvey (Lib Dem)	12,761		
Robert Batten (National Front)	2,470		
Total number of voters	**84,751**		

In defence of SV, it prevented the election of a Conservative who did not have majority support. Under FPTP, the Conservative candidate would have won, arguably because the centre-left vote was split between Labour and the Liberal Democrats.

However, the result also shows that SV cannot be relied upon to fulfil the main criterion of majoritarian representation: the Labour candidate was still elected without the support of most voters. This was because only 10,398 of the 15,231 second preference votes were cast for either of the remaining candidates.

Prospects of electoral reform: enhanced or diminished by 2005?

The 2005 general election has prompted all the main parties to ponder the Westminster electoral system.

Labour: disenchanted with reform?

Simply on grounds of self-interest, Labour's yearning for electoral reform for Westminster has withered. Why?

- As shown above, Labour does extremely well out of FPTP and does not want to lose its capacity to govern alone.
- Relations with the Liberal Democrats (with whom Labour might have to govern under PR) have cooled since Charles Kennedy became Lib Dem leader. In large parts of the north, Labour and the Liberal Democrats are implacable enemies.
- Labour is already hurt by PR in the Scottish Parliament, which has forced the party into coalition with the Liberal Democrats and resulted in embarrassing policy U-turns (notably on student tuition fees).
- There has been no public clamour for reform.

However, Labour's pro-reformers, like Peter Hain, warn that FPTP in 2005 will heighten people's cynicism towards politicians — and Labour could become exclusively identified with a discredited system. A hung parliament at the next general election is not unlikely and might cause another shift in Labour's attitude. For Labour to cling on to power in a hung parliament, a deal with the Liberal Democrats might be needed — and that would almost certainly include an overhaul of FPTP.

Conservatives: time to rethink?

In the wake of the 2005 election, there is more interest in electoral reform among Conservatives. In restating his support for PR, Lord Patten indicated 'growing support' among Conservative MPs, including senior figures like David Willetts, Kenneth Clarke and new party leader David Cameron (*Daily Telegraph*, 17 September 2005). This new interest is not hard to explain:

- As indicated already, the party received more votes in England than Labour — but 93 fewer seats.
- In Wales, it received almost twice as much support as Plaid Cymru — but only the same number of seats.
- As John Curtice warned, the ineffectual spread of Tory support means that, even if the party received more votes than Labour, it could still have fewer seats. For the Tories to gain a majority of seats, they might need a vote lead of up to 11% over Labour.
- Thanks to PR, the Tories have sizeable representation in the Scottish Parliament and the Welsh Assembly; under FPTP, they would have been virtually absent. The devolution elections have raised the Tories' profile in Scottish and Welsh politics and, as such, they have recovered from the 'meltdown' of 1997, gaining three Welsh seats in 2005.

Yet Conservatives have traditionally supported FPTP and are still generally wary of reform. For them, the key issue is that it would increase the chance of a hung parliament — and in hung parliaments, small parties seem more likely to coalesce with Labour. In short, for the Tories to govern, they have to govern alone and only FPTP offers this possibility. That said, if the Tories fail again in 2009 or 2010, they may conclude that a share of power is the best they can hope for. This will mean not just a new view on electoral reform but a whole new approach to politics — one that will make them more amenable to smaller parties, particularly the Liberal Democrats. David Cameron and shadow chancellor George Osborne are said to be particularly aware of this reality, so there may be a subtle shift in the Tory party's attitude in the next few years.

Liberal Democrats: still hurting?

The Liberal Democrats unequivocally favour proportional representation, seeing it as vital to the restoration of UK democracy. But they also have a strong vested interest: the Liberal Democrats can only hope to govern through a coalition, and coalitions are almost certain under PR. Indeed, the use of PR for Scottish Parliament elections has already produced a Lib–Lab coalition — even though the Liberal Democrats came only fourth in terms of votes. This, in turn, has raised their credibility in general elections. It is significant that, while the Liberal Democrat vote rose nationally by 3.8%, in Scotland it rose by 6.3%.

It is worth stating, though, that FPTP is not hurting the UK's third party quite as much as it once did. For example:

- The third party polled 3% fewer votes in 2005 than in 1983, but received almost three times as many seats.
- In Wales, the Liberal Democrats polled fewer votes than the Tories in 2005, but won more seats.

The Liberal Democrats' improving fortunes under FPTP have come about because its support is rather more concentrated than it was 10 years ago. In many southern and suburban areas, the party has established itself as the main anti-Tory force and therefore benefited in 1997 and 2001 from increased tactical voting. But it has also been boosted, in many parts of the north, by a raised profile in local government and its emergence as the main alternative to Labour.

Nonetheless, the Liberal Democrats still had a raw deal at the 2005 general election. Their share of MPs was 12% lower than their share of the vote, and despite getting more votes than Labour in the southeast, they received 13 fewer seats. With the flaws of FPTP now more vivid than ever, they plan to intensify their campaign for reform in the years ahead.

Conclusion: what's going on?

To complete this survey of the modern electoral system, it is worth recalling three remarkable facts:

- Between 2003 and 2005, voters in Wales and Scotland were subjected to three different electoral systems.
- Between 2004 and 2005, voters in Greater London were subjected to four different electoral systems. Indeed, in June 2004, they were subjected to three different systems *on the same day*!
- In no other democracy in the world is there such a variety of electoral systems.

UK electoral systems, 2003–05

- *First-past-the-post (plural representation).* This was used in the 2005 general election to elect MPs and the UK government. It was also used in the council elections of 2003–04 to elect local authorities in England and Wales.

- *Closed party list (proportional representation).* This was used in the 2004 European elections to elect MEPs from England, Wales and Scotland.

- *Additional member system (proportional representation).* This was used to elect the Scottish Parliament and the Welsh Assembly in 2003 and the London Assembly in 2004.

- *Single transferable vote (proportional representation).* This was used to elect the Northern Ireland Assembly in May 2003 and Northern Ireland's MEPs in June 2004. It will be used in Scottish council elections from 2006.

- *Supplementary vote (majoritarian representation).* This was used to elect the London mayor in 2004 and the mayors of four other English towns in 2005.

Little wonder that, according to some, the government has made a mess of electoral reform: by confusing voters with an array of electoral systems, the government has left them even more alienated from UK politics. Far from reviving representative democracy — the alleged intention of electoral reformers — electoral reform may have achieved the precise opposite.

The reported comment of one London voter, faced with three different ballot papers and three different voting methods, was 'what the hell's going on?' (*Evening Standard*, 10 June 2004). We should remember that, despite the flaws of FPTP exposed in 2005, electoral reform can be — and has been — hazardous. The chaos that followed the German PR election in September 2005 should serve as a reminder that other electoral systems simply carry other sorts of problems. In the end, it is a case of deciding which set of problems is the most serious — and that depends on your politics and the sort of government you would like to see.

Summary

- The 2005 general election brought FPTP into disrepute.

- *But* its avoidance of a hung parliament, and the chaos wrought by the subsequent German election, show that FPTP still has vital strengths.

- The debate hinges on what electoral systems are *for*: 'strong' single party governments or 'proportionate' parliaments?

- The answers to that question are influenced by the vested interests of the political parties.

- Doubts now exist as to whether FPTP *does* guarantee 'strong' government via the avoidance of hung parliaments — especially if Labour ceases to be the most popular party.

- Following the 2005 general election, a hung parliament seems quite likely: if the anti-Labour swing of 2005 is repeated in 2009 or 2010, no party will have a majority.

- A hung parliament under FPTP (giving the Liberal Democrats the balance of power) would dramatically increase the chances of electoral reform.

- There is growing interest in reform among Conservatives.

Chapter 2

The 2005 general election: how the UK voted

About this chapter

The 2005 general election was a prime opportunity to view the state of voting behaviour in the UK. This chapter will answer the following questions:

- How important is social class in determining voting behaviour?
- Why do people vote as they do?
- Why was turnout low?
- How important was the campaign?

OK, so what happened?

Before attempting any analysis of the 2005 general election, you should appraise the basic information contained in Table 2.1.

A cursory inspection of voting patterns in 2005 shows a huge difference from those of the 1950s and 1960s. That was a period of electoral 'alignment', when

Party	Total votes	Vote share (%)	Change in vote (%)	Seats	Change in seats	Candidates
Labour	9,547,876	35.2	−5.5	355	−47	627
Conservative	8,772,599	32.3	+0.6	197	+33	630
Liberal Democrat	5,982,164	22.1	+3.8	62	+11	626
UK Independence Party	602,498	2.2	+0.7	0	0	496
Scottish National Party	412,267	17.7*	−2.4	6	+2	59
Green Party	257,717	1.0	+0.3	0	0	162
Democratic Unionist Party	241,856	33.7*	+11.2	9	0	18
British National Party	192,746	0.7	+0.5	0	0	119
Plaid Cymru	174,836	12.6*	+1.7	3	−1	40
Sinn Fein	174,530	24.3*	+2.6	5	+1	18
Ulster Unionist Party	127,414	17.8*	−9.0	1	−5	18
Social Democratic and Labour Party	125,626	17.5*	−3.5	3	0	18

*Refers to vote share in Scotland, Wales or Northern Ireland respectively.

Other seats were won by George Galloway (Respect), Peter Law (Independent), Richard Taylor (Kidderminster Hospital and Health Concern) and Michael Martin (Speaker).

Table 2.1 Main general election voting figures, 2005

most voters were firmly attached to either Labour or the Conservatives on the basis of social class, and any shifts in voting behaviour had a nationwide character.

Of course, it must be remembered that changes in voting patterns had been evident at most elections since 1970 — a period usually termed the 'era of dealignment'. But the 2005 election offered particularly strong evidence that voting behaviour today bears little resemblance to that of 40 years ago.

Partisan dealignment

At the start of the election, YouGov discovered that only 38% of voters considered themselves 'firm supporters' of any one party. Consequently, we were to witness some startling swings in support. These are exemplified in Table 2.2.

Constituency	Swing
Blaenau Gwent	39.7% fall in Labour support
Brent East	24.4% fall in Labour support
Birmingham Sparkbrook and Small Heath	21.4% fall in Labour support
Ynys Mon	11.5% fall in Conservative support
Bethnal Green and Bow	10.1% fall in Conservative support
Burnley	10.1% fall in Conservative support
Ryedale	11.6% fall in Lib Dem support
North Southwark and Bermondsey	10% fall in Lib Dem support
Torbay	9.6% fall in Lib Dem support

Table 2.2 Some sizeable swings, 2005 general election

Diminished class voting

During the 1980s, Patrick Dunleavy remarked that 'when predicting how people will vote, knowing their social class — information once so crucial — is now about as useful as tossing a coin'. There was further evidence for Dunleavy's claim in 2005, when almost two thirds of middle-class (ABC1) voters did *not* back the Conservatives and almost 60% of working-class voters did *not* back Labour (see Table 2.3).

	Middle class	Working class
Labour	33% (−3)	41% (−7)
Conservative	36% (−0.3)	29% (+0.3)
Liberal Democrat	24% (+3)	20% (+3)

Table 2.3 Class voting in 2005 (change from 2001 in brackets)

Another notable aspect of Table 2.3 is that, although the Conservatives' overall share of the vote rose, support fell away among their 'natural' middle-class supporters. Likewise, the drop in Labour's support was greater among working-class voters than middle-class voters; almost all the double-figure falls in Labour support occurred in seats where blue-collar workers form a majority. This was the case for the three examples in Table 2.2.

Diversity of party support

A consequence of this breakdown in class voting is greater support for those parties with no class connection. The Liberal Democrats have arguably been the main beneficiaries of this, gaining more votes than Labour in southern England and more votes than the Tories in northeast England and Scotland. However, other 'classless' parties prospered as well:

- The SNP, with 18% of the votes, gained more votes and seats in Scotland than the Tories.
- Plaid Cymru won as many seats in Wales as the Tories.
- The Greens saved deposits (i.e. won more than 5% of votes) in 19 constituencies and came third in Brighton Pavilion with over a fifth of the votes.
- The British National Party saved 34 deposits and came third in Barking, just 60 votes behind the Tories.
- George Galloway's Respect Party took the seat of Bethnal Green and Bow from Labour and came second in a further 3 seats.

In addition, independent candidates were elected in Blaenau Gwent and Wyre Forest.

Again, it must be emphasised that these multi-party trends were evident before the 2005 general election. UKIP, for example, came third in the 2004 European elections and third in the Hartlepool by-election later that year, polling more votes than the Conservatives.

Chapter 3 expands upon the diversification of party support.

Diverse voting patterns

On the night of the 2005 general election, the BBC again deployed its customary 'swingometer', but apart from theatricality it was hard to see what purpose it served. For example, quite early on, the result from Putney showed a 6.5% swing to the Tories — a result that, if repeated in other marginal seats, would have seriously threatened Labour's majority. Yet it quickly became clear that this would not happen. Within minutes of the Putney result, the result from Cheadle (another key marginal) showed a swing *away* from the Conservatives of 4% — a zigzag pattern seen throughout the night.

Although there was a slight swing to the Conservatives nationally, Table 2.4 shows that, in northern England, Tory support *receded*. It also reveals that the anti-Labour swing varied markedly from region to region, from 3.4% in the southwest to 8.4% in London.

Even within regions there were marked variations of swing. In north Wales, for example, the Tories took Clwyd West on a 1.3% swing from Labour, but in Ynys Mon (Anglesey), the Tory vote collapsed by 11%. In north London, the

Tories took Enfield Southgate on a swing of 9%, yet achieved virtually no swing at all in the neighbouring seat of Enfield North. In short, one could say that the voting patterns of 2005 were virtually pattern-less.

	Labour	Conservative	Liberal Democrat	Nationalist
Northeast	−6.6	−1.8	+6.7	
Northwest	−5.6	−0.6	+4.6	
Yorkshire and Humberside	−5.0	−1.1	+3.5	
East Midlands	−6.1	−0.2	+3.1	
West Midlands	−5.9	−0.1	+3.9	
Eastern	−6.9	+1.5	+4.4	
London	−8.4	+1.4	+4.4	
Southwest	−3.4	+0.1	+1.4	
Southeast	−5.0	+2.1	+1.7	
Scotland	−4.4	+0.2	+6.3	−2.4
Wales	−5.9	+0.4	+4.6	−1.7

Table 2.4 Regional trends in party support, 2001–05 (%)

Low turnout

At just 61.5%, turnout in 2005 was the second lowest in a general election since 1918, and only 2% higher than in 2001. In certain constituencies, turnout was even lower, as Table 2.5 shows. The causes of low turnout are examined on p. 13.

Constituency	Turnout (%)
Liverpool Riverside	41.4
Manchester Central	43.1
Salford	43.3
Glasgow Central	44.1
Liverpool Walton	44.5
Kingston-upon-Hull West	45.0
Kingston-upon-Hull East	45.2
Glasgow North East	45.9
Manchester Gorton	45.9
Leeds Central	46.2

Table 2.5 The 'terrible ten': lowest constituency turnouts, 2005 general election

Class dealignment

Underpinning all these changes, perhaps, is a less class-conscious and more varied society. A YouGov poll published in early 2005 (*Daily Telegraph*, 3 January) showed that a majority of voters no longer see themselves as either working or middle class, defining themselves according to lifestyle, consumer choices, ethnicity, gender or sexuality.

The causes of class dealignment are complex, but the effects are simple: if voters no longer identify with the two traditional classes of society, they are unlikely to identify with the two class-based parties. As a result, voters become more volatile, more likely to vote for 'other' parties, less likely to conform to any national pattern, and — as we saw in 2005 — less likely to vote at all.

Why so little interest?

For many commentators, low turnout has been the defining feature of the last two general elections. It is not, of course, a purely UK malaise, but why is it so virulent in this country? Just after the 2005 election, a YouGov poll detected the following reasons:

- *'They're all the same.'* There is a perception that the main parties are locked into an unhealthy consensus, making general elections irrelevant to the policies of the government.
- *'Even if they wanted to change things, they couldn't.'* Voters are becoming aware that UK politicians are hemmed in by forces largely beyond their control, such as global economic forces, EU regulations and the sheer power of markets.
- *'They'll say one thing but do another.'* Politicians, it seems, are increasingly viewed as sleazy and untrustworthy; the recent fall of David Blunkett may have confirmed these suspicions.
- *'Government is remote from our area's interests.'* Despite the current government's support for devolution, there is a belief that decisions are taken by distant elites in the Westminster/Whitehall 'village'.
- *'The result was a foregone conclusion.'* In both 2001 and 2005, there was little chance Labour would lose, so voting may have seemed pointless.
- *'In my constituency, the same party always gets in anyway.'* Some caution is required here because some of the highest turnouts in 2005 were in safe Tory seats (90% in Hampshire East). Nevertheless, the 50 constituencies with the worst turnout were generally safe seats.

What made people vote the way they did?

But what are the factors guiding those who *do* vote? With psephology so complex, a range of explanations now merit attention.

Tribal affiliation

Despite partisan dealignment, there are still plenty of voters — maybe a third, according to YouGov — who see themselves as staunch supporters of a political party. With the non-tribal electorate increasingly turned off, this shrunken body of 'core' voters could yet decide the outcome of a general election. Indeed, the Tory strategy in 2001 and 2005 was based on the belief that the Tory 'core' would outnumber Labour's and that the Tories could thus win on a low turnout. This strategy is now discredited, but we should not overlook the large number of voters who still have an emotional, and often class-based, attachment to their party.

From tactical voting to 'tactical unwind'

The phenomenon of tactical voting has two sources. First, it is suggested that, with voters less inclined to liking any party, they will more probably be swayed by *dislike* of one party in particular — and to vote in the way most likely to ensure its defeat.

Second, it could be argued that voters who do have a strong party allegiance are now more 'clued-up' about its prospects in their constituency. If it has no chance of winning, they are more likely to vote for whichever party might defeat the party they like least.

There was strong evidence of tactical voting in both 1997 and 2001, when plenty of voters were driven by contempt for the Conservatives but, in 2005, there was a tail-off — a trend John Curtice terms 'tactical unwind'. This would help to explain why the Tories gained 35 seats, despite their overall vote share rising by just 0.6%.

Anger at Blair's government meant that Liberal Democrat supporters, in particular, were less willing to vote for Labour. This produced the sort of Tory gains shown in Table 2.6, which gives the results for the Shipley constituency. The Tory vote actually receded in Shipley, but because the Liberal Democrat vote rose — mainly at Labour's expense and in a seat the Liberal Democrats had no chance of winning — the Tories took the seat.

	Votes in 2001	Votes in 2005
Labour	20,243	18,186
Conservatives	18,815	18,608
Liberal Democrats	4,996	7,018

Table 2.6 'Tactical unwind': the case of Shipley

Likewise, in the south the Tories regained some seats from the Liberal Democrats and avoided losing others, possibly because Labour voters were less prepared to switch to the Liberal Democrats. In Western-super-Mare, for example — a Liberal Democrat marginal and a prime venue for tactical voting if Labour supporters wished to defeat the Tories — Labour's vote fell by just 1%, despite falling by 3.4% in the southwest region generally. The result was a Tory gain. All this may have had something to do with the Liberal Democrats' relentless attacks on Labour after 2001; Charles Kennedy, in particular, has shown much less interest in future Lib–Lab deals than his predecessor, Paddy Ashdown.

How important was 'issue-based' voting?

Labour's supremacy may have something to do with the fact that it is still considered more competent at dealing with the issues that voters consider important. The key issues in 2005, according to YouGov, are listed in Table 2.7. As Table 2.8 shows, Labour had a lead in four of these top six issues.

Which of the following issues will be most important when you decide how to vote?	
Health	18%
Taxation and public services	13%
Law and order	14%
Education	15%
Economy generally	14%
Asylum and immigration	11%

Table 2.7 Key issues, 2005

Which party is putting forward the best policies on...	Labour (%)	Conservatives (%)	Liberal Democrats (%)
Health	37	23	14
Taxation and public services	31	25	17
Law and order	30	31	11
Education	32	24	16
Economy generally	41	22	11
Asylum and immigration	24	35	12

Table 2.8 Issues and party ratings

Which issues drove the campaign?

The figures shown in Tables 2.7 and 2.8 were released at the start of the 2005 campaign. The central task for Tory campaigners was to raise the saliency of the two issues on which their party was strong: law and order, and immigration.

For Labour, the aims of the campaign were:
* To neutralise the issues of law and order, and immigration, by showing its own 'toughness' in these areas.
* To protect its lead on the four other issues. For Labour, it was especially important to highlight its reputation for sound economic management, as this was once an area where the Tories prevailed. This explains the key role that Chancellor Gordon Brown was given in Labour's campaign.

For the Liberal Democrats, the main aim seemed to be attracting disgruntled Labour voters by highlighting:
* Liberal Democrat tax plans, including a 50% tax rate for those earning over £100,000 p.a., which would fund, among other things, a raise in the state pension.
* Their plans to scrap council tax in favour of local income tax.

- Their opposition to the Iraq war.
- Their opposition to student tuition fees.

Did the campaign make a difference?

Voters' views about key issues and the party best placed to tackle them changed little throughout the campaign. Neither did opinion polls show much change in Labour's lead over the Tories. For that reason, Labour's *damage limitation* campaign may be judged a success, and the Tory *core vote* campaign a failure.

Labour's campaign may have retarded the Liberal Democrats' *decapitation* strategy, which was designed to unseat prominent Tories by encouraging Labour voters to vote Liberal Democrat. Labour's message during the final week of the campaign, that a vote for the Liberal Democrats would 'let the Tories in', may have divided the anti-Tory vote in southern marginals, thus aiding the survival of Tories such as Oliver Letwin.

The failure of the Tory campaign was even more remarkable given two events during the campaign that should have helped their cause:
- The news that MG Rover was going into receivership, bringing into question Labour's stewardship of the economy.
- The conviction of terrorist Kamel Bourgass, strengthening the Tories' claim that there is a link between the terror threat and Labour's asylum policies.

By contrast, Liberal Democrats could take some comfort from their campaign. Opinion polls recorded an average 2% increase in Liberal Democrat support during the campaign, mainly from voters disenchanted with Labour. The following reasons can be offered for this development:
- The Liberal Democrats' stress on Old-Labour-style 'tax and spend' may have helped in seats with high numbers of deprived working-class voters. Hence their gain in Rochdale and their staggering increase in support (22%) in both Birmingham Ladywood and Birmingham Hodge Hill.
- Their opposition to the war in Iraq, reinforced during the campaign by the release of Lord Goldsmith's report (mildly critical of the government's conduct leading up to the war), helped the Liberal Democrats in seats where there was a significant Asian population. In the 50 constituencies with the highest Muslim population, the Lab–Lib swing averaged 8.5%.
- Their attack on tuition fees seemed to pay dividends in seats where there was a high number of students — the best example is Manchester Withington, taken from Labour on a swing of 17%.

Are age and gender significant?

Age is a much bigger factor in voting behaviour than it was 30 years ago. Between 1950 and 1970, we could never have said that the result of a general election would have been different if voting had been confined to those within a 20-year age range. But we *can* say this about the 2005 election. As Table 2.9 shows, if the electorate had been confined to over-55s, the Tories might well have won a majority seats.

	18–34	35–54	55+
Labour	37	41	32
Conservative	28	29	41
Liberal Democrat	27	22	40

Table 2.9 Voting by age group, 2005 (%)

Further evidence of a widening generation gap can be gleaned from a comparison with the 1997 general election, when Labour had a lead in *all* age groups, including those aged over 65.

In 2005 there were again signs of a gender gap in voting behaviour. Even in the era of alignment, there was some evidence of this, although it was slight and tended to involve women — even working-class women — being more disposed to vote Conservative.

Since 1997 this has been reversed, and it is notable that in 2005 Labour's lead over the Conservatives among women voters was three times greater than its lead among men (see Table 2.10). A breakdown of gender voting by age is even more revealing. Of those aged 18–30, Labour did 7% better among women than among men. Furthermore, among middle-class women aged 25–55, Tory support fell by 4% despite rising by 4% among middle-class men of the same age.

	Men	Women
Labour	35	38
Conservative	33	32
Liberal Democrat	23	23

Table 2.10 The gender gap: voting by gender, 2005 (%)

To explain these trends, the Tories might remember that, among younger women, there are a growing number of careerists (who may perceive the Tories as a traditional, 'woman's place is in the home' party) and single parents who may recall the Major government's 'Back to Basics' campaign, with its stress on 'traditional family values' and the importance of marriage. Small wonder that some senior Tories, like party chairman Francis Maude, have since recommended the 'feminisation' of the party (via all-women shortlists for parliamentary candidates) and a more explicit endorsement of alternative family structures.

Harder to explain is declining Labour support among older voters. More than any other section of the electorate, these voters have a vested interest in high public spending, fairly high taxes and generous state provision — ideas to which Labour has a stronger ideological attachment than the Tories.

Conclusion

For students of psephology, there was nothing particularly extraordinary about the 2005 general election: most of its key features were already evident by 1983. The chief characteristic of voting behaviour remains voter volatility and detachment from any of the main parties. Although the headline result — Labour's election for a third term — may suggest stability and alignment, the underlying trends point to an electorate increasingly hard to predict.

Summary

- Voting behaviour in 2005 was consistent with theories of dealignment.
- There were huge variations of swing.
- Tactical voting receded.
- Voters are susceptible to new parties and maverick candidates.
- The issue of why people vote for a party is now rivalled by the issue of whether they vote at all — and, if not, why not.
- There are no clear signs of realignment: with the demise of class voting, it is still hard to predict how an individual will vote.

Chapter 3

The 2005 general election: towards a new party system?

About this chapter

Since the 1970s, there has been doubt about the true nature of the UK's party system. This chapter will address key questions following the 2005 general election:

- Is the two-party system still intact?
- Has a three-party system been cemented?
- Have the Liberal Democrats peaked?
- Do new parties like Respect embed a multiparty system?
- Does New Labour's third term mark a dominant-party system?
- Is there, in fact, no clear party system in UK politics today?

Still a two-party system?

For much of the postwar era, the UK had a universally recognised two-party system, the features of which are outlined in the box below.

The traditional party system

- **A duopoly of electoral support**. Only two parties, Labour and the Conservatives, had sizeable voter support. In the general election of 1951, for example, they polled 97% of the votes cast.

- **A duopoly of parliamentary representation**. Only two parties had sizeable numbers of MPs. After the 1951 election, all but nine MPs were Labour or Tory.

- **A parity of electoral support**. The two parties regularly polled over 40% of votes cast, and the average vote gap between them was just 3%.

- **A parity of power**. With such substantial support, both parties looked capable of winning general elections. Between 1945 and 1970, the Tories governed for 13 years and Labour for 12 years.

- **A nationwide two-party battle**. In the bulk of constituency contests (in 1951, all but 12) Labour and the Tories took first and second places.

- **Sizeable support nationwide for the two main parties**. At the 1955 general election, the Tories were the most popular party in Scotland (with 36 MPs), while Labour, though defeated, still won 42 seats in southern England.

- **An electorate stable in its support for the two main parties**. Large swings of support were rare (never higher than 5%) and about 80% of voters identified, long term, with the Labour or Conservative parties. The reason for this was…

- **A strong link between the two main parties and the two main social classes**. About 65% of the working class regularly voted Labour and about 75% of the middle class regularly voted Tory. 'Classless' parties, like the Liberals, naturally struggled.

Following the 2005 general election, it was clear that there were still some traces of the old two-party system in modern UK politics:

- **Two parties still have the bulk of parliamentary seats**. Labour and Tory MPs make up 85% of the House of Commons.
- **There was renewed parity of electoral support**. The vote gap between the two main parties (3.2%) is now virtually identical to the average gap between 1945 and 1970.
- **There was limited support for other parties** — none of which managed even a quarter of votes cast. Indeed, the third party's vote share was 3% lower than in 1983.
- **The second party made some recovery**. As indicated above, a two-party system needs more than one party capable of victory and, after 2005, the Tories claimed to be 'back in business', for reasons outlined in the box below.
- **There is still a link between the two parties and the two main social classes**. The Conservatives were still the most popular party among middle-class voters, while Labour still had a clear lead among working-class voters.

The Tories in 2005: the road to recovery?

- The Tories are now just 3% behind Labour in terms of votes (the figure was 12% in 1997).

- The Tories were the most popular party in England.

- They made a net gain of 33 seats, even winning seats in Wales and west Yorkshire — areas where they were once thought 'extinct'.

- If they make similar progress at the next election, they will strip Labour of its majority.

- The Tories are second in 27 of the 33 seats that Labour must hold to stay in power in 2009 or 2010, and in 80 out of 100 of Labour's most marginal seats, thus reinforcing the Lab–Con nature of the next general election's battle-ground.

A comprehensive survey of the Conservative Party's position appears in Chapter 5.

A dead two-party system?

Like most elections since 1970, the 2005 general election still pointed to a party system very different from that of the 1950s and 1960s (see Table 3.1).

Election	Conservatives Vote share (%)	Seats	Labour Vote share (%)	Seats	Liberal* Vote share (%)	Seats	Other Vote share (%)	Seats	Turnout (%)
1970	46.4	330	43.0	288	7.5	6	3.1	6	72
1974 (Feb)	37.8	297	37.1	301	19.3	14	5.8	23	78
1974 (Oct)	35.8	277	39.2	319	18.3	13	6.7	26	73
1979	43.9	339	37.0	269	13.8	11	5.3	16	76
1983	42.4	397	27.6	209	25.4	23	4.6	21	73
1987	42.3	375	30.8	229	22.6	22	4.3	23	75
1992	41.9	336	34.4	271	17.8	20	5.8	24	78
1997	30.7	165	43.2	418	16.8	46	9.3	30	71
2001	31.7	166	40.7	412	18.3	52	9.6	29	59
2005	32.3	197	35.2	355	22.1	62	10.4	31	61

*'Liberal' denotes Liberal Party 1970–79; SDP–Liberal Alliance 1983–87; Liberal Democrats 1992–2005.

Table 3.1 Party share of votes and number of seats, 1970–2005

The following points suggest that the 2005 election signalled the death of the two-party system:
- A third of voters backed neither Labour nor the Tories. At 67.5%, the combined vote of the main two parties was the lowest ever at a general election, with neither party managing even 40% of votes. This fall-off echoed other recent UK elections: in the 2004 European elections, the two-party vote was only 59%.
- There are now 92 MPs from parties other than Labour and the Tories — the highest figure since 1923.
- The winning party won only 35% of the total votes — the lowest figure ever recorded for a party with a majority of seats.
- The main opposition party won only 32% of votes and fewer than 200 seats. These figures suggest that we are not poised for a wholesale change of government in the style of a classic two-party system.
- It is no longer a nationwide two-party contest. Labour and the Tories were not the two most popular parties in Scotland, the northeast and the south outside London. In a total of 219 constituencies, the second-placed party was neither Labour nor the Tories.
- The two main parties do not have substantial support nationwide. Labour won less than a quarter of the votes in the south outside London. The Tories have only 1 out of 59 seats in Scotland and 3 out of 40 seats in Wales; they have no seats in the northern cities of Manchester, Liverpool, Sheffield, Leeds and Newcastle.

- The electorate is not stable in its support for the two parties. Like the Tories in 1997, Labour suffered from some huge swings against the governing party, for example a 40% swing in Blaenau Gwent and a 24% swing in Brent East.
- The link between the two parties and the two main social classes has diminished. A majority of middle-class voters did not vote Tory and a majority of working-class voters did not vote Labour.

A three-party system?

Selected Liberal Democrat gains, 2005

Rochdale (northwest)	Cambridge (East Midlands)
Taunton (southwest)	Solihull (West Midlands)
Hornsey and Wood Green (London)	East Dumbartonshire (Scotland)
Leeds North West (Yorkshire)	Cardiff Central (Wales)
Withington (Greater Manchester)	

For Liberal Democrat leader Charles Kennedy, the 2005 general election 'cemented the three-party system' and represented a 'huge landmark' for the UK's third party. Why?

- The Liberal Democrats won a record number of seats — 62 MPs (a net gain of 11) represents the highest Liberal Democrat total since the party was formed and the biggest number of third-party seats since 1923.
- The Liberal Democrats won most of the support that Labour lost. With a 3.8% vote increase from 2001 (compared to just 0.6% for the Tories), the Liberal Democrats were the main beneficiaries of the 5.5% drop in Labour support.
- The Liberal Democrats made gains in all parts of the country (see the box above). As such, the UK's third party — once dismissed as a party of the 'Celtic fringe' — now has a truly national character.
- In many urban areas, the Liberal Democrats are the main opposition to Labour. The UK's third party won more votes than the Tories in Scotland, northeast England, Manchester, Liverpool and Sheffield. The Liberal Democrats took 12 urban seats from Labour in 2005 (e.g. Rochdale) and have more seats than the Tories in Scotland, Wales, Manchester, Leeds, Sheffield and Birmingham (see Table 3.2).
- In many suburban and rural areas, the Liberal Democrats are the main opposition to the Conservatives. The UK's third party won more votes than Labour in the south (outside London), and in the southwest received more votes and won more seats than Labour. The Liberal Democrats gained 3 Tory seats in 2005 (e.g. Taunton) and increased their majorities in ex-Tory seats, such as Cheadle in the north and Romsey in the south.

	Labour		Conservatives		Liberal Democrats		Nationalists	
	Vote share (%)	Seats	Vote share (%)	Seats	Vote share (%)	Seats	Vote share (%)	Seats
England	35.5	286	35.7	193	22.9	47	17.7	6
Scotland	38.9	40	15.8	1	22.6	11	12.6	3
Wales	42.7	29	21.4	3	18.4	4		
Southeast England	24.4	19	45.0	58	25.4	6		
Southwest England	22.8	13	38.6	22	32.6	16		
London	38.9	44	31.9	21	21.9	8		
Northwest England	45.1	61	28.7	9	21.4	6		
Northeast England	52.9	28	19.5	1	23.3	1		
Yorkshire and Humberside	43.6	44	29.1	9	20.7	3		
Eastern England	29.8	13	43.3	40	21.8	3		
West Midlands	38.9	39	34.8	15	18.6	3		
East Midlands	39.0	25	37.1	18	18.5	1		

Table 3.2 Main party performance in the British regions, 2005

A stalled three-party system?

Despite these achievements, there were some who felt after 2005 that the Liberal Democrats had lost momentum and that the UK's three-party system had 'stalled'. The following reasons may be cited for this view:

* The third-party vote share was lower than it was in the 1980s (see Table 3.1).
* The third-party vote total was lower than in three previous general elections: the Liberal Democrats won more votes in their first ever general election of 1992, while the Alliance won more votes in the 1980s.
* The Liberal Democrats made limited progress in the south: outside London, they added less than 2% to their 2001 vote, while their 'decapitation' strategy, designed to unseat prominent Tories, was a failure. Some Liberal Democrats were concerned that the party's centre-left policies allowed Tories to recoup southern support. As a result...
* The Liberal Democrats lost 5 southern seats to the Tories, including Guildford and Newbury. This raises further doubts about whether the growth of a three-party system is relentless and inevitable.

Has the Liberal Democrat bubble burst?

In the words of *The Times* writer Peter Riddell, the Liberal Democrats in 2005 'could and should have done better', for the following reasons:

* An unpopular government, seriously undermined by its policies on Iraq, student tuition fees and a growing reputation for mendacity, meant that many centre-left voters were reluctant to vote Labour.

- The Conservative opposition still lacked credibility. Indeed, its renewed 'core vote' strategy could have repelled many centre-right voters. As such, Charles Kennedy's claim that the Liberal Democrats were the only 'real alternative' to Labour had resonance.
- The increased Liberal Democrat presence in local government, their success in by-elections between 2001 and 2005 (e.g. Brent East 2003, Leicester South 2004), and the telegenic presence of their leader meant the party did not lack profile.

These factors led some Liberal Democrat strategists to forecast gains of 70–80 seats. But they ended up with 11. Why? There are several possible explanations:

- *Lacklustre leadership?* Even during the campaign, there were complaints among Liberal Democrats that Kennedy was too laid back and insufficiently proactive in his leadership. Kennedy later admitted that he had been 'more like a chairman than a leader'. When party politics is in flux, emergent parties need leaders who are dynamic and urgent — as George Galloway showed with Respect.
- *Flawed tactics?* By galvanising Tories in many of the Liberal Democrats' target seats (like Michael Howard's), the high-profile nature of the Liberal Democrats 'decapitation' strategy backfired. Among southern, centre-right voters, the strategy seemed to confirm the Liberal Democrats as a centre-left, anti-Tory party rather than a more comforting, catch-all centre party.
- *The electoral system?* A YouGov poll indicated that a vote for the Liberal Democrats is still perceived by a third of voters as a 'wasted vote' (*Daily Telegraph*, 30 April 2005). As such, the party is still suffering a double whammy from FPTP: because of its past failures to convert Liberal Democrat votes into seats, the system is now stopping the party's support from being converted into votes.
- *A lack of clarity?* The same YouGov poll also found that over half of those questioned were 'unsure what the Liberal Democrats stand for'. Sometimes, of course, this can work to the party's advantage, allowing voters to use the Liberal Democrats as a 'protest' party, without being aware that some of its policies might offend them. But if the party is to move onto a higher level of support, as it hoped to do in 2005, it may need a more distinctive and clearer philosophy to which voters can relate more positively. The party might be reluctant to adopt one, for fear of alienating some of the diverse 'protest voters' it currently attracts.

Despite winning the highest number of third-party seats since the 1920s, the mood at the 2005 Liberal Democrat party conference was one of mild disappointment rather than jubilation — a vindication of Riddell's analysis. Among delegates, there was anxiety that a major breakthrough would now be harder to achieve for the following reasons:

- *Iraq.* The war cost the government huge support among people who were normally Labour voters (especially Muslims), which the Liberal Democrats were able to exploit thanks to their own anti-war position. Iraq may be nothing like as salient an issue by 2009 or 2010.
- *Blair.* By 2005, the prime minister had come to personify the UK's involvement with Iraq, its close relationship with President Bush and its growing reputation for lies and 'spin'. But Blair will not be leading Labour into the next election, and the Liberal Democrats could be hampered by the presence of a new prime minister — especially if it is Gordon Brown, who is thought to have more empathy with the Old Labour voters Liberal Democrats try to woo in certain areas.
- *The Tories.* Under David Cameron, the Conservatives might also be rejuvenated by 2009 or 2010. The Tories hope that by the next election voters' memories of the Major government will be more distant, while its young leader will be determined to win back support lost to Liberal Democrats in southern and suburban areas.
- *Internal divisions.* At the 2005 Liberal Democrat conference, there were signs of growing division and confusion among party members. Modernisers like Mark Oaten and Vince Cable, who hope to push the party towards a more free-market, Eurosceptic position, met fierce opposition from conservatives like Lord Greaves and Simon Hughes. These doctrinal squabbles seem unlikely to abate and could make the party less effective and attractive in the years ahead.

A multiparty system?

Peter Kellner claims that the two-party system is dead and that there is now a multiparty system, with more than one party benefiting from the problems of the 'big two'. The 2005 general election offered clear evidence in support of this analysis:

- There are now MPs from 10 different parties: the 'big three' plus the SNP, Plaid Cymru, the DUP, the UUP, Sinn Fein, the SDLP and Respect. There are also two independents: Peter Law (Blaenau Gwent) and Dr Richard Taylor (Wyre Forest).
- There are now a record number of MPs (31) from 'other' parties (see Table 3.1).
- There were candidates from over 100 parties. Many of these were no-hopers, yet deposits were still saved by the candidates of 24 different parties. They are listed in Table 3.3.
- In Scotland, the SNP won more votes and seats than the Tories. It is worth noting that Scotland has MPs from four different parties (the 'big three' plus the SNP).
- In Wales, Plaid Cymru won as many seats as the Tories. Wales, too, has MPs from four different parties (the 'big three' plus Plaid Cymru). Wales's

multiparty system was neatly illustrated by the contest in Ceredigion, where the Liberal Democrats took the seat from Plaid Cymru.

- UKIP increased its share of the vote, saving its deposit in 37 constituencies (it came third in Boston and Skegness).
- The Green Party saved 19 deposits (it came third in Brighton Pavilion).
- In its first general election, Respect won one seat (George Galloway in Bethnal Green and Bow) and came second in four other seats (e.g. West Ham). Four out of 21 other Respect candidates saved their deposits.
- The far right again progressed. The British National Party quadrupled its total vote to almost 193,000; it was only 27 votes off second place in Barking and saved a total of 34 deposits.
- Mayoral elections. The four mayoral elections of 2005 reinforced multiparty tendencies. In Hartlepool, the independent mayor was re-elected, in Doncaster an independent was runner-up, and in Stoke-on-Trent the BNP and the Supporting Green Shoots Party each polled over 15,000 votes.

Party	Best share of vote (%)	Constituency
Green Party	22	Brighton Pavilion
British National Party	17	Barking
Alliance Party	15	East Antrim
Scottish Labour Party	14	Glasgow North East
Liberal Party	12	Liverpool; West Derby
UKIP	10	Boston and Skegness
Community Action Party	8	Makerfield
Scottish Green Party	8	Glasgow North
Operation Christian Vote	8	Western Isles
Community Group	7	Doncaster North
Veritas	6	Erewash
Scottish Socialist Party	6	Orkney and Shetland
Socialist Alternative	5	Coventry North East

Table 3.3 Minor parties with candidates who saved deposits, showing their most successful constituency(ies)

As explained in Chapter 1, the 2005 results increased pressure for reform of the electoral system. Judging by the effects of new voting systems for the UK's European elections and devolved bodies, any reform to the Westminster system would advance not just the Liberal Democrats but many smaller parties.

A dominant-party system?

In a dominant-party system, a number of parties may compete for votes, but only one wins enough to gain office. Dominant-party systems are therefore marked by long spells of government by one party. With three consecutive election wins for New Labour, coming after four for the Tories, there are signs

of such a system in the modern UK. Labour's dominance seems entrenched by two factors:

(1) Weak and divided opposition. Labour's main rivals, the Conservatives, are still beset by an identity crisis and few assume that they will be ready for power by 2009 or 2010. Moreover, as we have seen, the anti-government vote splits a number of ways, allowing Labour to 'divide and rule'.

(2) The electoral system. As shown in Chapter 1, the electoral system is heavily biased in Labour's favour. The party could get a majority of seats with just 29% of votes and up to 3% fewer votes than the Tories. Indeed, Labour in 2005 obtained a majority of 65 with just 35% of votes (in 1992 the Tories had a majority of only 21 with 41% of votes).

However, after the 2005 election, one should be cautious about saying Labour is dominant:
- Labour was backed by only 22% of eligible voters.
- Its share of the vote was higher in 1979 — when it lost.
- Its total vote was higher in 1987 and 1992 — when it lost.
- Its total vote was lower than the Tories achieved in 1997 — when *they* lost.
- It polled only a quarter of the votes in southern England.
- It polled fewer votes than the Tories in England as a whole.

In short, Labour's dominance stems only from the vagaries of the electoral system and the chronic weakness of its main opponents.

By-elections: a clue to the UK's party system?

The two by-elections held in 2005 — Cheadle in July (following the death of Liberal Democrat MP Patsy Calton) and Livingstone in September (following the death of Labour MP Robin Cook) — are a helpful guide to the nature of the modern party system. The results of each election are given in Table 3.4.

Cheadle (14 July)			
M. Hunter (Lib Dem)	19,593	52%	(+3%)
S. Day (Con)	15,936	42%	(+2%)
M. Miller (Lab)	1,739	4.6%	(−4%)

About 300 votes were cast for three other candidates.
Lib Dem majority: 3,657. Turnout: 55%. Swing: 0.6% Con to Lib Dem.

Livingston (29 September)			
J. Devine (Lab)	12,319	42%	(−9%)
A. Constance (SNP)	9,639	33%	(+12%)
C. Dundas (Lib Dem)	4,362	14%	(−1%)
G. Lindhurst (Con)	1,993	7%	(−3%)

About 700 votes were cast for five other candidates.
Lab majority: 2,680. Turnout: 38%. Swing: 10% Lab to SNP.

Table 3.4 Parliamentary by-elections, 2005

What implications can be gleaned about the UK's party system from these first two by-elections of the 2005 parliament?

A renewed two-party system?

The Conservative performance does not point to any definite recovery of a two-party system, in which two parties are capable of winning a general election outright. In this respect, the Tories' failure to recover Cheadle is highly significant. When the Tories were last in government, they held Cheadle with a majority of 16,000. With a Liberal Democrat majority of 33 in 2001, it was the Tories' top target seat at the 2005 general election. Their failure to regain an affluent, suburban seat like this does not suggest the Tories are on course for power. In Livingston, the fact that they slipped by 3% and almost lost their deposit highlights the party's still marginal position in Scotland and other parts of the country — again, scarcely a portent of winning power. It is also worth noting that, in the eight by-elections since 2001, the Tories have failed to win any, and have only managed second place in two.

A strengthened three-party system?

The Liberal Democrats' success in Cheadle strengthened their claim that the UK — or at least England — now has a three-party system. Their success in holding on to the seat shows them to be well established in many suburban constituencies, displacing Labour as the main alternative to the Tories. However, the Livingston result proves that disenchantment with the 'big two' does not just benefit the third party.

A continued multiparty system?

The 10% swing to the SNP in Livingston, with the Tories trailing Labour, the SNP and the Liberal Democrats, confirms that in many Scottish and Welsh seats there are more than three 'serious' candidates seeking election.

A renewed dominant-party system?

The dominant-party system does not rest easily with either by-election. In Cheadle, Labour failed even to retain its deposit, the result showing that the UK's governing party is almost irrelevant in many rural and suburban contests. In Livingston, Labour's majority was slashed from nearly 14,000 to under 3,000, suggesting once again that Labour has a fragile grip on voters' confidence.

A variable party system?

The result of the two by-elections actually support Anthony King's thesis that the UK has no single party system but a *variety* of party systems. The box below offers a guide to this thesis.

But even this analysis, which suggests that the party system differs from region to region, is a simplification. In Greater Manchester, for example, there were fierce Con/Lab battles in Bury and Bolton; close Lib/Lab battles in Rochdale and Withington; and tight Con/Lib contests in Cheadle and Hazel Grove. All this points to a certain conclusion.

The variable party system

- Midlands, East Anglia and most of London: mainly Lab/Con contest.
- Northern urban areas: mainly Lab/Lib Dem contest.
- Rural and southern suburban areas: mainly Con/Lib Dem contest.
- Scotland: mainly three-way Lab/Lib Dem/SNP contest.
- Wales: often a four-way Lab/Lib Dem/Plaid Cymru/Con contest.

Conclusion: a vanished party system?

The word 'system' implies certainty, regularity and a relentless pattern of events. In the 1950s and 1960s, there was indeed a systematic feel to party competition, exemplified by the Labour–Conservative dominance throughout the country and the uniformity of swing from one constituency to another.

However, party support since then has been marked by irregular, and spectacular swings, and infinite fluctuations. In other words, the old two-party system has not been replaced by anything systematic. So, far from being reshaped, the UK's party system may have simply disappeared.

Summary

- The UK's party system is very different from that of the 1950s and 1960s.
- The UK's third party is much stronger today than it was 40 years ago.
- Evidence of a three-party system is not as clear-cut as Liberal Democrats would have wished before the 2005 general election.
- Other parties have also benefited from the decline of Labour and the Conservatives, prompting talk of a multiparty system.
- Among experts, there is no consensus about the type of party system now present in the UK.

Is UK democracy in crisis?

About this chapter

Developments between 2004 and 2005 confirm that traditional UK democracy — representative democracy — is not in robust health. This chapter addresses key questions about UK democracy in 2005:

- Is low turnout a result of disenchantment with political parties?
- What are the causes of disenchantment?
- Are pressure groups and protest movements the new forms of democracy?
- Do pressure groups in 2005 strengthen or subvert democracy?
- Are referenda the democracy of the future?
- Is representative democracy, with all its problems, still the best option?

Representative democracy in the UK, 2005: a faltering system?

Democracy in the UK has mainly taken the form of *representative democracy*: we elect MPs, governments, MEPs, councillors and so on to make accountable decisions for us. By 2005, this system of democracy did not look healthy.

Diminished turnout

An obvious yardstick, when inspecting representative democracy, is people's willingness to choose their representatives in elections. During 2004–05, it was depressingly clear that people were less and less willing to do so.

At the 2005 general election, only 61.5% of eligible voters cast their votes — the second worst turnout in a general election since 1918 (in 2001 it was 2% lower). This means that, as in 2001, the number of people who abstained was greater than the number voting for any political party, including the party that now governs us. Indeed, only 21.6% of the electorate supported Labour — a record low for a governing party. In many inner-city constituencies, only a minority voted. This is a worrying sign that society's 'have-nots' are now disconnected from our system of representative government. Among first-time voters, fewer than 40% chose to vote.

The less than impressive turnout in mayoral elections since 2001 (average 35%) and the Scottish and Welsh devolution elections (average 53% and 43%) is also significant, as it suggests that the restructuring of representative democracy will have only limited impact upon voter engagement.

Election	Date	Turnout (%)
Hartlepool parliamentary by-election	November 2004	43.0
General election (average)	May 2005	61.5
Liverpool Riverside (general election)	May 2005	41.4
Manchester Central (general election)	May 2005	43.1
Stoke-on-Trent mayoral election	May 2005	50.8
Hartlepool mayoral election	May 2005	51.1
North Tyneside mayoral election	May 2005	61.4
Doncaster mayoral election	May 2005	54.4

Note: turnout was probably inflated in the four mayoral elections by the fact they were held on the same day as the general election. In previous mayoral elections for these areas, turnout had averaged 35%.

Table 4.1 Selected election turnout figures, 2004–05

Are parties the problem?

Integral to UK representative democracy are *political parties*. After all, the representatives we elect are overwhelmingly party-based representatives; when we choose a government, it is usually on the basis of which party either impresses or annoys us. So if people are disenchanted with political parties, they are implicitly disenchanted with our whole system of representative government. By 2005, it was clear that disenchantment with parties was huge. This is shown by the following factors:

- **Diminished party identification**. Forty years ago, about four fifths of voters identified with one of the two major parties. A YouGov poll in May 2005 showed that only a third do so today. A majority of those questioned agreed that 'the main parties did not represent my interests' and were 'remote from the concerns of everyday life'. A staggering 61% thought that most party politicians were 'liars'.
- **Diminished party membership**. Figures released at the start of 2005 indicated that Labour's membership had fallen from 400,000 in 1997 to 170,000 today. The Conservative leadership contest of 2005 revealed fewer than 200,000 Tory members, suggesting a 25% decline since the leadership contest of 2001 — a far cry from the 1950s, when the party had over 3 million members. Although there has been some increase in the membership of other parties, research at Sheffield University in late 2004 showed that only 2% of adults are now members of a political party.
- **Ageing party membership**. Sheffield's studies also showed that party membership has become alien to young people. The average Labour member is now 55, while the average Conservative member is now 68. The two parties' youth movements have fewer than 30,000 members between them.
- **Growth of non-party voting**. There has been a tendency among voters to shun *all* political parties by voting for independents who decry all the major parties. At the 2005 general election, this was reflected in the election of Richard Taylor (Wyre Forest) and Peter Law (Blaenau Gwent), while in the mayoral elections of 2005 the independent mayor of Hartlepool was

re-elected, with an independent candidate coming a close second in Doncaster.

- **Growth of non-party politics**. Running parallel to the decline in party activity has been a surge in pressure group and protest activity. Among young voters in particular, movements like Make Poverty History and the Live8 concert seem much more rewarding forms of political engagement than that offered by political parties.

What causes disenchantment with representative democracy?

Disenchantment with representative democracy can be attributed to several factors, which are outlined below.

Sociological change: the decline of deference

Representative democracy involves trusting elites to determine what is best for us. Yet, in society as a whole, there is much less deference towards elites and authority of any kind (ask any parent, policeman, teacher or soccer referee). The repeated barracking of Tony Blair during the general election of 2005 was an obvious symptom of this. In a *New Statesman* article of February 2005, Martin Jacques cited a new 'karaoke culture', in which ordinary people were increasingly empowered and self-confident, less willing to entrust issues affecting them to others, and more likely to make their own individual arrangements (see the box below). Representative democracy, by its very nature, is at odds with these vital social trends.

A non-dependency culture?

Tim Evans of the London School of Economics released the following data in 2005:

- Thirteen million people now have private medical provision.
- In 2004, 250,000 people had self-funded surgery.
- Twelve per cent of parents now choose independent education.
- Thirty per cent of children in state schools receive private tuition.
- There has been a 32% fall, since 1970, in numbers depending on public transport.

Sociological change: class dealignment

Party-based representative democracy flourished at a time when most voters identified with a social class and, therefore, with one of the two parties representing those classes. YouGov found in January 2005 that 69% of voters now considered themselves 'classless' and therefore somewhat disconnected from the two main parties. As we shall see later (pp. 33–34), a more diverse society is now drawn to a more diverse form of political activity.

End of socialism/Cold War

Political parties deal in generalities, such as how society as a whole should be governed, and therefore seem relevant during periods when there is argument about what sort of society we should have. Until the late 1980s such an argument existed, principally between those who supported a more socialist society, based on public ownership, and those who defended a society run on capitalist lines. The end of the Cold War marked the end of that argument and the entrenchment of market–capitalist values. As a result, there is now less argument about the general nature of society and much more argument about specific issues within society — arguments that pressure groups are better equipped to address.

Parties 'all seem the same'

Following on from the previous point, it is now harder for the main parties to distinguish themselves with grand, radical visions of society. Reflecting the position of most voters, there is now a general acceptance of a 'social market', combining private ownership and consumer choice with high public spending and extensive public services. All the parties can do, it seems, is to present themselves as the best 'managers' of such a society — and voters are not easily enthused by managers.

Parties seem disempowered

Even if parties were to offer a radically different society, it is now doubtful that they could bring it about. More than ever, parties in government are hemmed in by factors beyond their control, such as a globalised market economy. Parties in government have contributed to this by relinquishing a series of vital responsibilities: since 1997, interest rates have been determined mainly by unelected officials at the Bank of England; since the 1980s, public services have been increasingly run by private companies; since the passing of the Human Rights Act in 1998, human rights have been increasingly defined by unelected judges; and since the 1970s, responsibility for huge areas of economic, transport, environmental and immigration policy have been ceded to the European Commission in Brussels.

Voters may therefore have concluded that political parties — and therefore our whole network of representative democracy — can no longer 'make a difference'. Little wonder, then, that many voters have sought other channels for political change. This tendency has been strengthened by the reputation for 'sleaze' now surrounding party politicians, underlined in 2005 by the confessed misconduct of ex-Home Secretary David Blunkett.

Pressure group politics: a new form of democracy?

In late 2004 and 2005, there was further evidence that the politically engaged were turning from parties to pressure groups and protest movements. That said, the difference between parties and pressure groups is still often blurred. Many so-called parties contesting the general election, for example, had a single-issue character and therefore no real interest in governing (see the box below).

Parties or pressure groups?

'Parties' contesting the 2005 general election included:

- Build Duddon and Morecambe Bridges
- Croydon Pensions Alliance
- Families First
- Independent Kidderminster Hospital and Health Concern *(held Wyre Forest)*
- Not In My Name
- Legalise Cannabis Alliance
- Motorcycle News Party
- People of Horsham First Party
- Publicans/Free to Smoke Party
- Save Bristol North Baths Party
- Wessex Regionalists Party

It is tempting to argue that democracy in the UK has assumed a pressure-group-led character. Three particular pressure groups had a conspicuous effect on political debate in 2005:

- **Make Poverty History**. Timed to coincide with the G8 summit at Gleneagles in July, and designed to alert world leaders to the continuing problem of African poverty, its apogee was the Live8 concert in Hyde Park (see p. 35).
- **Countryside Alliance**. In late 2004, this group responded vigorously to the government's bill banning fox hunting. Its most newsworthy activity came when some of its members, such as Otis Ferry, stormed the floor of the House of Commons in order to remonstrate with MPs.
- **Fathers4Justice**. Created to champion the rights of estranged fathers, this group staged a number of spectacular, and eccentric, protests designed to highlight their cause. In February 2005, for example, protestors attired in *Star Wars* costumes sat on the roof of Manchester Town Hall to address bewildered onlookers.

However, it must be emphasised that these three groups were just the tip of a huge iceberg. The *Parliamentary Services Guide to Pressure Groups*, published annually, listed no fewer than 17,000 'significant' organisations in 2005, having cited just 4,000 when it was first published in 1981. In other words, 2005 confirmed what Rob Baggott termed, in a lecture given in January of that year, 'a relentless and exponential growth of pressure group activity in UK politics'.

Why has there been such a growth of pressure groups?

Pressure group activity has expanded for several reasons:

- **A more diverse society**. A YouGov poll at the start of 2005 showed that most people no longer define themselves as either working class or middle class, but in a much wider range of ways (e.g. gender, ethnicity, lifestyle,

consumer choices). The multitude of pressure groups reflects this multitude of interests.

- **A more affluent and communicative society**. An *Economist* social trends survey in May 2005 noted that, since 1997, levels of consumer spending had 'soared'; the number of people in further education had risen by a third; and almost half of all households now had access to the internet. Free from the worries of poverty, and with access to more information than ever, members of such a society are more likely to protest about issues that don't directly concern them (as with Live8). Furthermore, the spread of e-mail and mobile phones makes it easier for people to co-ordinate their own protest activities, unrestrained by distant bureaucracies — a factor exploited by both Fathers4Justice and the Countryside Alliance.

- **A weak opposition**. Since 1997, the chance of Blair's government being ousted has looked slim. In 2005, certainly, the Tories were not believed likely to win the general election. Some have therefore tried to alter the specific policies of the government rather than the government itself. As the *Daily Telegraph* remarked in late 2004, many Countryside Alliance members were 'natural Conservatives who despaired of the Conservative Party'.

- **A limited government mandate**. Protestors have been emboldened by the fact that only 22% of voters supported the government at the general election, thus weakening its mandate to implement controversial policies — a point made by various civil rights pressure groups (in response to the ID cards bill) and trade unions (in response to plans for further privatisation of public services).

- **The 'politics of particularism'**. This was the phrase used by Wyn Grant to describe the political climate following the end of both the Cold War and the more general dispute between capitalist and socialist values. The heightened concern about such issues as fox hunting, fathers' rights and African poverty all point to a society that has resolved its own basic values and which becomes, as a result, more concerned with specifics.

Do pressure groups strengthen democracy?

Pressure groups can be said to *benefit* democracy in the following ways:

- **Pressure groups enhance political participation**. As described earlier, there has been a startling fall in the number of people active in political parties. But pressure groups have corrected this by allowing huge numbers to become more directly involved in the political process between elections. For example, over 22,000 people attended the Live8 concert in London, and up to 30,000 took part in various Make Poverty History marches in the days that followed.

- **Pressure groups enhance parliamentary democracy** — mainly by ensuring that MPs have a more informed view before debating key issues. The fox-hunting debate in the Commons, for example, was enriched by the links that many MPs had with both the Countryside Alliance and various animal rights groups.

- **Pressure groups are dynamic and responsive**. Unlike parties, which often seem sluggish in framing new policies, new pressure groups can immediately meet new political issues. Stop the War, formed in 2003 after the invasion of Iraq, is an outstanding example; August 2005 saw the emergence in the northwest of Muslims for Manchester, which was formed after the London bombings of July, and designed to show that 'most Muslims in Manchester have no links with violent, pseudo-Islamic groups' and 'identify fully with the multicultural, Mancunian community we live in'.
- **Pressure groups are often democratically organised**. At a time when parties are often accused of 'control freak' tendencies, some groups like to highlight their 'open' and 'grass-root power' organisations. Fathers4Justice, for example, held postal ballots for all its supporters in 2005 on policy declarations that it would submit to the government.
- **Pressure groups make a difference**. The Countryside Alliance claimed that, following its protests, the fox-hunting bill was more qualified than originally envisaged. The impact of the Make Poverty History (MPH) campaign can be gauged by the G8's decision to double aid to Africa and target the elimination of AIDS — a tribute to the huge profile given to these issues by MPH campaigning.

Make Poverty History: a case study in pressure group action

Between April and July 2005, MPH deployed a number of tried and tested pressure group tactics in pursuit of influence at the G8 summit in Scotland:

- *Celebrity backing.* The support of people like Bob Geldof, Bono and all those who performed at the Live8 concert in Hyde Park helped to raise awareness of African poverty, especially among the apolitical young.

- *Public engagement.* The Live8 concert itself popularised the cause by linking a serious political issue to public enjoyment.

- *Media attention.* Live8 led to huge, and largely free, media coverage of the MPH agenda.

- *Dialogue with ministers.* MPH celebrities used their profile to gain access to senior government figures, which allowed MPH to contribute to more measured and intricate discussion.

- *Dialogue with MPs.* Using what Geldof called a 'multi-track approach', MPH leaders also met with interested MPs, who were asked to put their own, parliamentary pressure on ministers.

Do pressure groups subvert democracy?

It can also be argued that pressure groups *undermine* democracy in a number of ways:

- **Pressure groups can obscure the 'silent majority'**. The government claimed, with reference to opinion polls, that the views of rural voters were more ambiguous than the Countryside Alliance suggested. In this situation,

pressure group influence could easily impede, rather than enhance, democracy.

- **Pressure group leaders do not always speak for pressure group members**. Linked to the previous point is the fact that not all pressure groups are member-led. The Automobile Association (AA), for example, cited its million-strong membership when lobbying the government (in March 2005) for a reduction in speed limits on motorways. But, as its literature admitted, this policy was framed by various AA 'councils' rather than a plebiscite of AA members.
- **Pressure groups can bring parliament into disrepute**. Debates in early 2005 concerning Private Finance Initiatives in the NHS gave the impression that many MPs, far from being constituency representatives, were simply acting as spokespersons for interest groups — be they private companies (in the case of many Tories) or trade unions (in the case of many Labour back-benchers).
- **Pressure groups oversimplify complex issues**. Make Poverty History, for example, gave the impression that the elimination of African poverty could be achieved by eight political leaders and ignored the fact that its causes were complex and sometimes lay with African governments. The type of politics associated with Madonna, Sting and Dido represent 'infantilisation' of debate, unlikely to produce sensible and mature decisions by government.
- **Pressure groups can encourage a narrow and selfish perspective on politics.** This was exemplified in 2005 by the National Union of Students' campaign against top-up fees, which was oblivious to the effects that 'free higher education for all' would have upon public spending — and therefore society at large. As one minister remarked (anonymously), 'In my day, students wanted to save the world. Now they just want to save themselves.'
- **Pressure groups can promote the 'politics of coercion'**. Some of the most conspicuous — and effective — pressure groups are those that promote public disorder and inconvenience. Between August and September 2005, animal rights campaigners forced the closure of Darley Oaks Farm in Staffordshire (it had been a vivisection clinic), while the posturing of the Fuel Lobby produced chaotic panic-buying at petrol stations. Given that democracy rests heavily upon the rule of law, these are not healthy developments.

Direct democracy: the democracy of the future?

In the aforementioned *New Statesman* article, Martin Jacques argues that UK democracy should 'reinvent' itself by moving towards extensive use of national and local referenda. Although we still await the first nationwide referendum since 1975, there have been, since late 2004, two significant referenda in specific parts of the UK. They are outlined in the box below.

UK referenda, 2004–05

■ **Edinburgh City Council area, February 2005**

Should the city council introduce a congestion charge for traffic entering the city centre?

Yes: 24%. No: 76%. Turnout: 62%.

■ **Northeast England (as defined by European elections), November 2004**

Do you accept the government's proposal for a regional assembly in the northeast of England?

Yes: 22%. No: 78%. Turnout: 48%.

In addition to these, there were two referenda abroad (in May 2005) that had immense implications for the UK: the French and Dutch referenda, on the proposed EU constitution. The resounding 'no' in both countries made it unlikely that the UK would have its own referendum on the constitution, even though the prime minister had made it sound almost inevitable a year earlier.

Did the 2005 referenda vindicate direct democracy?

The 2005 referenda supported the concept of direct democracy in several ways:

- *They reflected the particularisation of modern political debate.* As indicated during our survey of pressure groups, politics today is less concerned with the nature of society and more concerned with specific issues. Ballots on particular policies, such as congestion charges, fit in with this trend.
- *The Edinburgh ballot suggested some public yearning for direct democracy.* Turnout (62%) was marginally higher than UK turnout in the general election, indicating that ballots on everyday issues (common in the USA) could become fashionable.
- *The northeast ballot cemented the precedent for referenda on constitutional change.* Given the devolution referenda in Scotland and Wales (1997) and the 31 referenda on elective mayors (2001–04), it is now axiomatic that constitutional reform in the UK should involve direct democracy.
- *The northeast, French and Dutch referenda allowed voters to defy elites.* In all three cases, voters took the opportunity to ignore the advice of their governments — a victory for 'people power' and conducive to a more democratic political culture. In the case of the northeast ballot, the *Daily Telegraph* commented: 'It is an awesome result. The Yes campaign had everything going for it, supported by Labour, the Liberal Democrats, the regional trade unions, most regional newspapers, most local councils, the Mayor of Middlesbrough and numerous prominent businessmen' (6 November 2004).

Did the 2005 referenda undermine direct democracy?

On the other hand, it can be argued that the referenda of 2005 undermined the concept of direct democracy:

- *Turnout in the northeast ballot (48%) pointed to voter indifference.* It reminds us that, in general, voters are no more drawn to direct democracy than representative democracy. It is worth noting that by 2005 there had been 31 referenda on whether to have elective mayors and average turnout was under 40%. It should also be remembered that these ballots cost public money — £600,000 in Edinburgh, £11 million in the northeast — raising the question of whether this money would be better spent on vital public services.

- *Voters did not give due attention to the issue at hand.* An exit poll conducted by the *North East Times* showed that only 18% of voters had 'a fair understanding' of how the proposed regional assembly would work. Likewise, a poll for the French newspaper *Le Figaro* showed that voters had only a tenuous grasp of what the proposed EU constitution involved. Both papers suggested that ordinary voters had neither the time nor the inclination for careful reflection of the issues, implying that...

- *Voters voted on irrelevant criteria.* Polling evidence in 2005 showed that voters were using the referenda to make a broader political protest against those in power. On the EU constitution, the French left were said to have voted 'no' mainly to rebuff a right-wing president. Similarly, the 'no' vote in the northeast of England may have stemmed from a growing antipathy to the government (the region recorded a higher than average swing against Labour in the general election 6 months later). But if voters are approaching referenda in the same way as conventional elections — voting on the basis of parties and personalities rather than issues — we might as well stick to representative democracy.

- *Ambiguous questions yield ambiguous answers.* Critics of referenda have always cited their tendency to oversimplify complex issues and to reduce subtle debates to unsubtle yes/no questions. As a result, the message behind a referendum result is not always clear. For example, in France the 'non' was caused partly by French nationalists rejecting further European integration. But it was also caused by French leftists rejecting an 'Anglo-Saxon capitalist' Europe in favour of a more 'socialist' federation. Similarly, in the northeast, according to the mayor of Middlesbrough, many 'no' votes were a protest against the proposed assembly being a 'talking shop' as opposed to a body with more substantial powers. In other words, these referenda highlight the trickiness of public administration and vindicate full-time, representative politicians with the time and know-how to make measured decisions.

- *The fading prospect of an EU referendum in the UK points to governmental cynicism.* A perennial criticism of referenda is that their timing and wording are pregnant with party-political calculation. The government's likely refusal to go ahead with the EU referendum, despite effectively promising one a year earlier, stems from a fear that, like its French and Dutch counterparts, it would suffer a humiliating reproach. Yet, despite the EU constitution being 'dead in the water', there remains a strong case for a referendum in the UK — if only to clarify public opinion on the critical issue of European integration.

Democracy in the UK: a glaring paradox?

By 2005, UK voters were more affluent, aware and sophisticated than ever. As we have seen, this helped make them more cynical and critical of representative democracy — a system that presupposes a degree of deference and respect towards authority. It is unlikely that today's politicians are any less competent than their predecessors; it is just that the voters are more discriminating.

Affluence, awareness and sophistication reflect a society that is more hectic and dynamic. The demise of the traditional family, in which men had paid employment and women stayed at home, and the disappearance of an economy that offered jobs-for-life and regular hours, have thrown society into a sort of prosperous anarchy in which old role models no longer apply. The interests of society, once divided neatly into working class and middle class, are now multifaceted and much harder to discern. The issues that confront us, so clear during the Cold War era, now seem more oblique and confusing.

The point is this: there is now a particularly urgent need for parties and professional politicians in the UK to crystallise, and reconcile, the myriad forces affecting society. Single-issue protests can be healthy but they can also ignore the wider issues and consequences. Single-issue ballots also seem a good idea, until we realise that the mere phrasing of the question raises further political problems. And are voters, already frantically juggling their own lives, really equipped to contemplate and resolve matters such as the European single currency (an issue, incidentally, which divides professional economists)?

In short, representative democracy, where we entrust politicians to make decisions for us, may be more appropriate now than ever before. The problem is that voters think otherwise; and with all political systems resting, ultimately, on popular consent, that problem is not trivial.

Summary

- Representative democracy in the UK is in crisis.
- Low turnout in elections is a prime symptom.
- The unpopularity of political parties is another.
- The rise of pressure group/protest politics seems relentless.
- The extension of direct democracy looks inevitable.
- But these alternative forms of democracy carry problems.
- Representative democracy may still be the 'least imperfect' model.

Chapter 5

Party policy in 2005: consensus confirmed?

About this chapter

The year 2005 offered a prime opportunity to assess the policy and ideology of the UK's main political parties. This chapter will answer the following questions:

- Did the 2005 manifestos offer voters clear ideological alternatives?
- Did the 2005 general election result in the 'entrenchment of a centre-left progressive settlement'?
- What policy differences were there between the parties in 2005?
- Will a Brown leadership produce a return to traditional Labour policies?
- What are the prospects for the Liberal Democrats?
- Is there an emerging consensus on what a future Conservative government would do?
- Have we reached an 'end of ideology' in terms of UK party politics?

The 2005 general election: a Thatcherite consensus?

According to the *Guardian*'s Michael White, the main party manifestos of 2005 'embedded the post-Cold War, Thatcherite consensus', and offered voters 'merely a choice of Thatcherisms' rather than any 'clear, ideological alternatives'. In terms of fundamentals, all three major parties — Labour, Tories and Liberal Democrats — certainly shared a number of vital underlying principles that echoed the radical Tory governments of 1979–97:

Capitalism and market-based economics

Gone are the days when Labour, and to a lesser extent the UK's third party, questioned the utility of private enterprise. All three parties accepted that only markets, competition and the profit motive could deliver the prosperity that voters expected.

Low inflation, rather than full employment, is the 'holy grail' of economic policy

All the main parties nodded in the direction of job creation and the need to generate more employment opportunities. But they all accepted that this could not be achieved unless the currently low level of inflation (around 2%) was sustained.

The pursuit of low inflation should not be entrusted only to politicians

Gordon Brown's earliest decision as chancellor, to give 'operational independence' to the Bank of England in the setting of interest rates (allowing governments merely to give the bank an inflation figure target) was questioned by neither the Tories nor the Liberal Democrats — even though it spelt a huge loss of government control over economic management and a corresponding loss of political accountability.

The private sector should be extended

Privatisation, once a source of bitter inter-party dispute, is now seen as either desirable or inevitable. The Private Finance Initiative (PFI), unveiled by the last Conservative government, is now supported by New Labour, which aims to advance it into sensitive areas such as welfare — an idea reinforced by New Labour's very own version of privatisation, the Public Private Partnership (PPP) scheme. Conservatives questioned the detail of such schemes but not the principles, and seemed mainly concerned that private companies should not be too shackled by bureaucratic criteria. The Liberal Democrats seemed preoccupied with giving PFI and PPP greater 'efficiency' and 'public accountability', rather than questioning their inherent value.

Public services should no longer have a 'one size fits all' character

All three manifestos emphasised the need for greater 'choice' in areas such as education and healthcare. Labour's belief in reforms such as 'foundation hospitals' and 'specialist schools', offering a diversity of provision and enjoying a degree of freedom from central government, was upheld by both the Tories (hence their support for 'turnaround schools' and 'consumer-led hospital care') and the Liberal Democrats (hence their support for 'community hospitals' and 'skills academies').

The private sector can deliver vital public services

Linked to the acceptance of 'diversity' and 'choice' is a widespread recognition that private schools and hospitals should be 'partners', rather than rivals, to state provision. For example, Labour's manifesto spoke of more NHS-paid operations being done in the private sector; the Liberal Democrats argued that the contribution of many independent schools to special needs education should be encouraged and supported by government; and the Conservatives argued that the state should pay part of the cost of treatment in private hospitals, should patients choose to go private.

'Property-owning democracy'

Back in the early 1980s, the Tories' 'right to buy' scheme, which allowed tenants to buy their council houses, was bitterly opposed by opposition parties. But in 2005, both Labour and the Liberal Democrats endorsed loudly the sacred Tory principle of home ownership. Indeed, Labour promised to *further* the 'right to buy' idea with its 'Homebuy' scheme, making it easier for council and housing association tenants to get on the property ladder, while helping first-time buyers by raising the threshold of stamp duty from £60,000 to £120,000.

There is wasteful public sector spending

Responding to the Tory claim that about £35 billion of public spending was unnecessary and should be directed to 'front-line' services, Labour promised to implement the Gershon Review and effect £21 billion of savings. Likewise, Labour echoed the Conservative pledge to axe 235,000 'superfluous' civil service jobs by promising its own cull of 80,000 public sector positions.

Tighter immigration controls

A fear that the country was being 'swamped' was a vital feature of Margaret Thatcher's 1979 election campaign and was updated in the 2005 Tory manifesto, which promised a 'quota system' for UK immigrants. Labour sought to neutralise this issue by echoing the Tories' belief in an Australian 'points system', relating to the skills of would-be immigrants. The Liberal Democrats also promised to cap immigration, albeit in a more 'humane' fashion than the two main parties. All three parties clearly believed that asylum and immigration were urgent problems meriting tough (and some would say illiberal) responses.

A pro-American foreign policy

'Atlanticism' had been a key aspect of Tory policy after 1979. Despite its claim that Blair had misled the country about the reasons for toppling Saddam Hussein, the Conservative manifesto endorsed the government's Iraq policy and the neo-conservative justification for regime change in the Middle East. (The Liberal Democrats diverged somewhat from this consensus, as we shall see presently.)

The 2005 general election: a social market consensus?

It is true that much of the above analysis does point to a Thatcherite agenda. But these aspects of party policy do not tell the whole story. Indeed, as Matthew d'Ancona stated in the *Sunday Telegraph*, the 2005 election marked 'the defeat of Thatcherite neo-liberalism' and the 'entrenchment of a centre-left, progressive settlement'. This is often described as a 'social market' consensus, where capitalism is combined with extensive state intervention. The evidence for this is as follows:

Acceptance of European integration

Although the Conservatives continued to make Eurosceptic noises, their manifesto indicated that they were as committed to EU membership as the two other main parties. This is significant, as the modern EU, with its 'social model' of capitalism, stands as an alternative to the free-market model, aiming to harness, rather than liberate, market forces. As the pro-free market Adam Smith Institute has pointed out, the EU — with its plethora of regulations and continental tariffs — is a 'brazen obstacle' to global free trade and a laissez-faire economic policy; hence the broad support it has among left-wing European parties.

Acceptance of high public spending

All three parties were happy with levels of public spending that amounted to around 40% of gross domestic product — a figure considered monstrously high by neo-liberals. It is worth recalling that the figure in 1905 was 9%, so Tories plainly accept the phenomenal growth of government in the last century.

Commitment to even higher public spending

Both Labour and the Liberal Democrats have an innate belief that more public spending equals greater social justice. But it is worth pointing out that the Tories, who pledged to save £35 billion by cutting 'wasteful spending', promised to spend £23 billion of that saving on 'more productive investment' in public spending. That the Tories have accepted greater public spending as a priority (and therefore 'social market' capitalism) is made explicit by their manifesto (see the box below).

The Conservative manifesto, 2005

'We will spend the same as Labour would on the NHS, schools, transport and educational development and more than Labour on police, defence and pensions... . Over the period to 2011–12 we will increase government spending by 4% a year, compared to Labour's plans to increase spending by 5% a year.'

Fairly high levels of taxation

With Labour keeping within the income tax levels established by the last Tory government, it is often forgotten that the overall tax burden has risen by 4% since 1997, thanks to a series of other tax reforms (sometimes referred to as 'stealth' taxes). As we shall see, the Liberal Democrats had no qualms about supporting even higher tax rates to fund higher public spending. More striking, though, was the Tories' acceptance of the 'Brown settlement' — their own meagre tax reduction plans (see p. 44) meant that the overall tax burden would stay much higher than when they were last in power. When frontbencher Howard Flight implied more ambitious tax cuts at a later stage, he was sacked from the shadow cabinet and effectively forced out of parliament by the leadership. It is worth recording that the Tory manifesto promised: no reversal of Brown's hikes in inheritance tax and national insurance; no raising of the threshold for paying income tax at the higher rate (which Brown had frozen at 1997 levels, dragging thousands more into the higher tax bracket); and no return of the marriage and mortgage tax allowances that Brown had scrapped. A large part of the reason for these concessions is the Tories' acceptance of various New Labour reforms (see the box below). But small wonder the Adam Smith Institute accused the Conservative manifesto of 'selling out to big government'.

Conservative manifesto concessions to New Labour reforms

- Acceptance of the minimum wage.
- Acceptance of working tax credit.
- Acceptance of child tax credit.
- Acceptance of the winter fuel payment to pensioners.
- Acceptance of one-off payment of £200 towards pensioners' council tax.

What divided the main parties at the 2005 general election?

Having established that the main party policies often converge, it should be said there were still important areas of divergence.

Liberal Democrats — breaking the mould?

During their campaign, the Liberal Democrats happily fed the idea that the two main parties were indistinguishable. They accordingly stressed several areas where they took issue with both Labour and Tory policy — hence their manifesto's title, 'The Real Alternative'. The most important examples of this are contained in the box below.

Proud to be different: distinctive Liberal Democrat policies, 2005

- A new, higher rate of income tax — 50% — for those earning over £100,000 p.a.
- Replacement of the council tax with a local income tax.
- Free residential care for the elderly.
- Entry into the single European currency 'as soon as realistically possible'.
- Proportional representation for Westminster.
- An elective second chamber.
- Legislative powers for the Welsh Assembly.
- Withdrawal of UK forces from Iraq.
- Security and immigration policies 'more consistent with civil liberties'.
- Opposition to ID cards.

Taxation

The Tories' promise of £4 billion of tax cuts was described by the Adam Smith Institute as 'chickenfeed'; yet it still signified a distinctive, tax-cutting *aspiration* on the part of the Conservative Party. Indeed, the party hinted at further tax cuts once 'adequate public service funding had been resolved'. By contrast, Labour gave no indication that in its view the UK was over-taxed, while the Liberal Democrats gave the impression that the UK was actually *under*-taxed — hence its promise of a new higher rate of income tax.

Europe

On the issue of the single currency, Labour's policy remained unchanged: it would continue to apply its 'five tests' to determine the UK's suitability before polling the public in a referendum. Meanwhile, the Conservatives restated their opposition to the euro in principle, while Liberal Democrats continued to seek entry 'at the earliest opportunity'. The Tories also promised to restore the UK's opt-out from the European Social Chapter.

Higher education

Both the Tories and the Liberal Democrats opposed Labour's policy of student tuition fees in higher education. In addition, the two opposition parties were varied in their alternatives. The Conservatives promised to finance higher education by limiting the number of school-leavers entering university to 30% (scrapping Labour's target of 50%), while the Liberal Democrats respected the 50% figure but promised to fund it via the tax increases mentioned earlier.

Pensions

The Tories and the Liberal Democrats promised to restore the link between earnings and the state pension, while opposing Labour's plan to increase its Pension Credit Scheme (PCS). The scheme had been criticised for generating too much bureaucracy, while failing to ensure that pension credits reached the neediest pensioners.

Poverty

Labour's justification for the PCS, and the expansion of other means-tested benefits like child tax credit and Sure Start, reflected its commitment to the eradication of poverty. As poverty is usually defined in relative terms, this implies that Labour still has a residual, socialist belief in the redistribution of wealth and a greater equality of *outcome*. Conversely, Tories and Liberal Democrats concentrated on greater equality of *opportunity*: the gap between rich and poor was judged irrelevant as long as the lot of the poor was improved.

Law and order

The Conservatives opposed Labour's bill that made the incitement to religious hatred an offence and advocated the expansion of custodial sentencing; they also attacked Labour's early release scheme for offenders as an insult to the 'law-abiding majority'. The Liberal Democrats argued that 'far more' should be done to rehabilitate offenders, restating their belief that crime was a comment on society as well as offending individuals.

The constitution

Labour's taste for constitutional tinkering continued with a promise to codify conventions for the House of Lords, while reducing its powers of delay to 60 sittings. The Liberal Democrats attacked Labour's diminished interest in electoral reform at Westminster and regional devolution in England. The

Conservatives offered a more reactionary approach, promising to cut the number of MPs by 20%, while giving voters in Wales the chance to close down the Welsh Assembly via a referendum.

Change in the air?

Following a general election, political parties normally undertake a review of their policies. Post-election party conferences are a notable opportunity for this, and the conferences of 2005 involved plenty of ideological ferment.

The Labour conference

With Tony Blair's resignation as prime minister in sight, many Labour delegates were keener than ever to hear from his probable successor. Those on the left of the party were hoping that Gordon Brown would herald a return to traditional Labour policies, with the Blair era proving an ideological aberration. As the *New Statesman* reported (26 September), 'Activists believe that, under Brown, Labour will be coming home.' However, Brown's speech — in effect a Labour manifesto for the next general election — left many delegates frustrated:

- The chancellor did not call for an end to New Labour but for a 'renewal of New Labour'. He affirmed his support for the Private Finance Initiative and greater commercial involvement in the reform of public services, while restating the importance of 'choice' and 'diversity' in the public services (coded support for Blairite policies, such as foundation hospitals and city academy colleges).
- In fringe meetings, Brown robustly defended his 'iron discipline in fiscal policy', reminding delegates of the need for tight control of public spending and the avoidance of 'anti-enterprise tax policies': in other words, ruling out the sort of income tax rises for the 'rich' demanded by left-wingers.
- In a *Newsnight* interview, Brown rejected trade union demands for greater union involvement on company boards, stressing the importance of 'flexible labour laws' and 'modern working practices'. He also pointed out that, although combating poverty had been 'one of his prime objectives', it was harnessed to a 'firm belief in the enterprise culture and the centrality of a vibrant business climate'.

In short, Brown's comments at this year's Labour conference served only as a reminder that Labour has travelled far from its traditional, socialist territory — and that Brown offers no prospect of changing direction.

That said, there were signs that Labour's grass roots may not be so compliant in future. At the 2005 conference, the leadership only narrowly avoided defeat on pension policy (many delegates favoured compulsory employer contributions to workplace schemes) and labour relations laws (trade union delegates showed a thirst for the re-legalisation of secondary picketing). Even more telling was that Labour's ruling National Executive Committee refused to back the leadership in its dispute with the unions over secondary picketing.

It is worth remembering that the three biggest trade unions — the TGWU, GMB and Amicus — are about to merge into a 'super union' of 2.6 million members. This new union is expected to cast about 25% of the votes at Labour's conference and contribute about a third of Labour's routine income. With a decidedly left of centre, 'Old Labour' character, it may yet cause problems for the Blair–Brown project during Labour's third term.

The Liberal Democrat conference

In ideological terms, the Liberal Democrat conference was perhaps the most interesting, for it revealed a party unsure of its future path. There seemed to be two obvious schools of thought:

(1) Centre-right modernisers. These are represented by MPs like Vincent Cable, Mark Oaten, Norman Lamb and Nick Clegg, whose common views first surfaced in a series of 'orange book' publications in 2004. They argued that the party must accept the spread of market forces and show less faith in 'big government' and its various manifestations, such as higher income tax and European federalism. At the conference, they argued for the partial sell-off of the Royal Mail (floating a third of its shares on the stock market) and a cap on the EU's unreformed budget. The modernisers hint that they would not be averse to a Lib–Con coalition if the new Tory leadership is true to its promise of a more 'compassionate Conservatism'.

(2) Centre-left traditionalists. MPs like Simon Hughes and John Hemming claim that the party should cling to the 'radical' position adopted in its 2005 manifesto, proving that the Liberal Democrats still supported the 'progressive' ideas that New Labour had abandoned, such as higher income tax rates for the 'rich' and increased non-means-tested benefits. Noting that, in most Labour seats, the Tories are now in second place, they argue that Liberal Democrats are more likely to gain seats next time by toppling Tory MPs — and they are more likely to topple Tory MPs if they don't sound like them. They also claim that, if the Tories return to the centre under David Cameron, it is all the more necessary for Liberal Democrats to stake out distinctive territory — i.e. to the left of Labour.

The Conservative conference

Owing to the extraordinary 'talent contest' at the 2005 Tory conference, involving the five candidates for the party leadership, the Conservatives might have seemed deeply divided as they assembled in Blackpool. But, beneath the personality clashes lay an emerging consensus as to what future Tory governments should do:

- Reduce the overall tax burden.
- Curb the growth of central government spending.
- Revive the spirit of one-nation conservatism by addressing problems of urban deprivation and the breakdown of urban communities.
- Introduce 'localism', by which political power is transferred wherever possible to county councils and town/city councils, and the 'direct democratisation'

of key positions in each locality, such as chief constables and chief education officers.

- Support a 'new Europe'. Even pro-EU Tories such as Ken Clarke conceded that neither the single currency nor the proposed EU constitution was feasible during the next decade. All candidates stressed that enlargement of the EU into a 'looser' trading bloc should form the basis of party policy on Europe.

Viable alternatives?

Chapter 3 highlights the emergence of multiparty politics in the UK. Consequently, any inspection of party ideology should note the key principles offered by some of the UK's new or 'alternative' parties. A summary of their main policy positions, based on their 2005 manifestos, is offered below.

Scottish National Party

- Full independence from the UK Parliament — Scotland to become a self-governing nation within the EU.
- Exclusive access to 'Scottish oil' to form the economic basis of independence.
- Modest redistribution of wealth via progressive taxation.
- No ID cards in Scotland.
- Council tax to be replaced by a local income tax.
- An end to means testing of most benefits.
- Setting up a 'Scottish Centre for Reconciliation and Conflict Resolution, to promote peaceful alternatives to armed conflict'.

Author's observation: this is a party that has positioned itself to the left of Labour, influenced by the fact that most of its target seats are in urban, Labour constituencies with a high proportion of working-class voters.

Plaid Cymru

- Primary short-term objective: to upgrade the Welsh Assembly into a Welsh Parliament, with legislative powers greater than those currently enjoyed by the Scottish Parliament.
- Primary long-term objective: full independence from the UK Parliament; Wales to become a self-governing nation within the EU.
- Economic policy geared to wealth redistribution; suspicious of free markets and 'speculators'.
- 'Green-friendly' taxes.
- Council tax to be replaced by a local income tax.
- Renationalisation of railways.
- An end to PFI/PPP schemes.

Author's observation: apart from an interest in electoral reform and a passion for the Welsh language, Plaid Cymru (like the SNP) seems to replicate Old Labour values in its search for Old Labour support in Labour heartlands.

UK Independence Party (UKIP)

- Withdrawal from the EU at the earliest opportunity and a subsequent re-evaluation of all policy areas 'where the UK government is currently hidebound' — particularly agriculture, fisheries, transport, and health and safety issues.
- A simplification of the tax system and an end to Labour's 'labyrinthine' tax credits.
- The revival of local government via the traditional county council system.
- Continuation of the PFI/PPP schemes to improve health/education systems — but with local councils having more regulatory powers.
- 'Tougher and clearer' immigration and asylum controls, allied to support for existing laws against racial discrimination.

Author's observation: although UKIP resists attempts to place it on a left–right scale, claiming that national self-determination cuts across such an issue, there is little in its manifesto that appeals to the 'progressive' mindset. Its comments on 'social justice', for example, merely restate the importance of national governments being able to deal with relevant policies free of EU criteria. Consequently, UKIP seemed to be offering a variant of conservatism, while being anxious to distance itself from the far right (hence its support for existing laws against racial discrimination).

Respect

- Immediate UK disengagement from Iraq.
- A 'radical reassessment' of the UK's relationship with the USA and a 'more independent foreign policy'.
- A revision of immigration and asylum laws so as to 'restore the importance of compassion and human dignity'.
- A shift from 'hidden' to progressive taxation, with the introduction of a wealth tax.
- An end to PFI/PPP and 'bold increases' in government welfare spending.
- Cuts in the UK defence budget.

Author's observation: to a large extent, Respect is an anti-Iraq war pressure group, devoting a bigger percentage of its manifesto to foreign policy than any of the main parties. When allied to its stance on immigration and asylum, it seems clear that the party was pitching for ethnic minority (especially Muslim) support in urban areas. However, its leader, George Galloway, insisted that the party's main aim was to 'revive the socialist agenda that New Labour has betrayed'.

British National Party (BNP)

- An end to all immigration and asylum-seeking within the UK.
- Withdrawal from the war in Iraq and an end to the UK's 'stooge status' in relation to the USA.
- Withdrawal from the EU.

- A new emphasis on 'binding British values', underpinned by 'traditional morality'.
- State-financed repatriation of immigrants wishing to return to their country of origin.
- An end to 'political correctness' in schools.
- Increased public spending in the NHS/education and a 'curb on racketeering' through PFI.
- More 'stop, search and detain' powers for the police.
- Restoration of capital punishment for murder and treason.

Author's observation: there are clear echoes of fascism in the BNP programme, particularly its hint that the UK needs to restore values lost due to the internationalisation of politics and society. The BNP's suspicion of privatisation seems as great as Respect's, and its call for more state spending and intervention confirm that it is aiming mainly at white working-class voters 'bewildered by multicultural forces'.

Green Party
- Reform of the tax system so as to reduce the use of cars and air travel.
- These tax reforms to form part of a general strategy for reducing carbon emissions and atmospheric pollution.
- Closer integration with the EU, facilitating a transcontinental approach to environmental reform.
- Devolution of power to regional parliaments across the UK, plus proportional representation at all levels of government.
- Greater awareness via the education system of the need for a more eco-friendly society.

Author's observation: the Greens have an interesting overlap with the left wing of the Liberal Democrats (people such as Simon Hughes) and offer an alternative home for the radical middle class. Through PR they hope to gain the same influence as their sister parties in countries like Germany.

Conclusion: a healthy choice?

Although there is a wide choice of policy ideas among UK parties today, the fact remains that, among the main parties, there is a strong level of agreement about the foundations of our polity and society. Is this a good thing?

On the one hand, it could be seen as a healthy development, signalling that more than one party has gauged the public's general desire for a mixture of private enterprise and state provision. When there is a huge ideological gulf between the parties, as in the early 1980s, this may indicate that one of the major parties has misread the public's aspirations, thus reducing the realistic choice for voters.

On the other hand, this consensus fuels (or maybe causes) the voter apathy that now defines our elections. Among voters 'unlikely to vote' in 2005, surveys showed a clear sense that parties were 'all the same' and that the result of the general election was somehow irrelevant (see Chapter 2).

With governments increasingly hemmed in by global market forces and EU rulings, it is not easy for parties to 'step outside the box' and offer distinctive versions of how the UK should be. All they can do, perhaps, is offer very specific policy changes, rather than grand visions concerning the nature of society. In terms of party politics, the UK has perhaps reached the 'end of ideology'.

Summary

- The 2005 general election underlined the social market consensus.
- The Labour Party offered pro-market reforms that it would have decried even a decade ago.
- A Brown premiership is unlikely to mark a serious change of direction for Labour.
- The Conservatives are a long way from a true free-market agenda and will move even further away under David Cameron
- There is growing ideological tension within the Liberal Democrats.
- More than ever, policy debate at the 2005 general election represented the 'politics of particularism', devoid of any huge ideological schisms.

Chapter 6

The leadership battle: a turning point for the Tories?

About this chapter

The 2005 general election — like the previous two general elections — was followed by an instant battle for the leadership of the Conservative Party. However, the 2005 contest proved altogether more fascinating than its predecessors, given the preliminary skirmish over how the contest should be fought, a remarkable Tory conference and the meteoric rise of David Cameron. The contest led to a belief that the party has now 'grasped the nettle' and is poised to mount a serious challenge to Labour. This chapter will answer the following questions:

- What was Michael Howard's approach to the succession?
- Why was there a dispute over the rules of the contest?
- What happened at the 2005 Tory conference?
- Did the campaign change anything?
- Why did David Cameron win?

6 May 2005: old ground revisited?

Within an hour of the polls closing on 5 May, exit polls revealed that the Conservatives had again failed to win a general election. Within 24 hours of the polls closing, the party was again in the throes of a leadership contest — Michael Howard announced that, in failing to lead the Tories to power, he had 'screwed up', and in the interests of 'accountability' was resigning.

Howard's decision, despite being ostensibly honourable, did not meet with unanimous approval. Former party chair Lord Tebbit said it was 'the last thing we needed', recalling that the leadership resignations of 1997 and 2001 only compounded the party's problems. For Tebbit and others, the party needed a period of 'quiet reflection', focusing on issues and policies rather than personalities. But Howard, like Major and Hague before him, had other ideas.

Why mess with the rules?

For those seeking 'quiet reflection', Howard's decision was made worse by his desire to change the rules determining his successor. Howard's wish was supported by new party chair Francis Maude, who shared Howard's view that the existing rules (established by William Hague's 'Fresh Future' reform

The 1998 Tory leadership election rules

These rules were used to elect Iain Duncan Smith in 2001 and David Cameron in 2005.

- Tory MPs vote in a series of ballots.
- After each ballot, the bottom-placed candidate is eliminated.
- When only two candidates remain, the contest involves the votes of all Conservative Party members (300,000 in 2001; 250,000 in 2005).

package of 1998) had seriously damaged the party during and after their first tryout in 2001.

So why did Howard, Maude and other Tory 'modernisers' take such a dim view of present arrangements?

- *The present system allows the election of a leader who is not the first choice of MPs.* Howard reminded the party of its 'fundamental belief' in parliamentary democracy, and how this was at odds with a leader 'foisted' on MPs by extra-parliamentary activists.
- *The present system is costly and time-consuming.* The 2001 contest had taken about 2 months to complete. Maude said this created confusion and uncertainty, and it would be best to have a system that produced leaders in weeks rather than months.
- *The present system provides leaders liked by the party but not by the public.* Howard and Maude implied that party members were more extreme than party MPs and were therefore less likely to choose leaders attuned to voter opinion.
- *Iain Duncan Smith.* The brief leadership of IDS was thought to embody everything that was wrong with the 1998 system. Unlike his final rival in the 2001 contest (Ken Clarke), IDS never topped the poll among MPs and was elected by party members despite evidence that Clarke was more appealing to voters. Two years after his election he was deposed by Tory MPs, thus giving the impression that the party had wasted the 2001–03 period.

What did Howard propose?

Howard initially proposed an inversion of the 1998 reforms, whereby candidates with support from at least 10% of MPs would submit themselves to an 'indicative ballot' among members of the Tories' National Convention (the 633 constituency chairs plus 244 national and regional officers). The two most popular candidates to emerge would then go to a final ballot of MPs. That way, it was argued:

- The contest would be quicker (the National Convention is much easier to convene than the overall membership).
- A degree of party democracy would be retained.
- The final decision would again rest with the parliamentary party.

However, at a meeting of Tory MPs on 15 July it emerged that only Maude and former party chair Theresa May supported Howard's proposal, thus fuelling the claim that former 'iron man' Howard had turned himself into a 'lame duck' by his imminent resignation. MPs made it clear that they did not want to be hidebound by *any* ballot of the extra-parliamentary party and were only prepared to accept the 'advice' of grass root Tory members. In other words, they wanted to return to the situation before 1998, when only Tory MPs voted in leadership contests.

What did Howard do next?

Chastened, Howard met with senior officers of the MPs' 1922 Committee (notably its chair, Sir Michael Spicer) and drew up a revised proposal that proved more acceptable to the parliamentary party.

The final proposed reform

- An MP requires backing from 5% of other Tory MPs to be a candidate.

- Any candidate with more than 50% backing automatically becomes leader.

- Once candidates are known, constituency party chairs take soundings among their members, then pass on the two most favoured candidates to the 1922 Committee.

- The information is made known to MPs before their own voting begins, but they are free to ignore it.

- A series of MPs' ballots eliminate the bottom-placed candidate until a winner emerges.

To go through, this revised reform had to be approved by the party's Constitutional College (another feature of Hague's 'Fresh Future' reforms), which has two sections:

- the National Convention (described above)
- MPs, MEPs and front-bench peers

For any constitutional reform to be accepted, it has to be endorsed by two thirds of those eligible to vote in each section — an exacting requirement. In the case of this reform, the test came on 27 September, when the Constitutional College met in central London. The results are in Table 6.1.

MPs, MEPs, peers in favour	165 (67.5%)
Extra-parliamentary activists in favour	446 (58.4%)
Overall number in favour	611 (61%)
Ballot papers returned	1,001 (88%)

Table 6.1 Conservative Constitutional College: results of the ballot on the proposed leadership selection rules, 27 September 2005

As can be seen, there was a pro-reform majority among both sections of the Constitutional College. However, as the majority among activists fell short of a two-thirds majority, the proposal was defeated and the 1998 system preserved — a hard blow to both Howard and Maude. Some Tory MPs wondered if Maude's position was now untenable, given his failure to deliver a key element of the modernising agenda.

Why did the reform fail?

Opponents of Howard's reform voiced the following objections:

- To 'de-democratise' its leadership contests would make the party look even more removed from the sort of society it sought to govern. Throughout the country, and indeed much of the world, there was a movement away from elite rule towards the empowerment of ordinary people. Howard's reform could have highlighted the party's reputation as old fashioned and out of step with modern culture.
- By marginalising party members, it would be harder to recruit them — and the party's grass-root campaign in 2005 showed a desperate shortage of young, energetic activists.
- Howard's latest attempt at eroding intra-party democracy was, for many in the party, a 'bridge too far'. Constituency officials were still smarting from the fact that, before the general election, two constituency associations had been forced to deselect candidates after those candidates fell foul of the leadership — the most notable example being shadow cabinet member Howard Flight (Arundel and South Downs). The party was tired of Howard's high-handed manner, especially as his leadership had just proved electorally unsuccessful.
- Some Eurosceptics saw the proposal as an attempt to smuggle Ken Clarke into the leadership — the conventional wisdom then being that MPs were more forgiving of Clarke's pro-Europeanism. With hindsight, this was a baseless fear, as Clarke always had more support among activists than MPs.

Who were the candidates?

During July and August, it sometimes looked as if there could be up to a dozen leadership candidates — Theresa May, George Osborne, Tim Yeo, Edward Leigh, David Willetts and Alan Duncan were all said to be 'taking the pulse' of MPs. There were even rumours that William Hague was up for a second crack at the job. Among senior MPs, only Oliver Letwin explicitly ruled himself out.

However, by the end of September, only five candidates emerged with nomination forms signed by fellow MPs:

- David Cameron (shadow education secretary)
- Kenneth Clarke (former chancellor)
- David Davis (shadow home secretary)
- Liam Fox (shadow health secretary)
- Sir Malcolm Rifkind (former foreign secretary)

Who were the favourites?

A YouGov poll in June (*Daily Telegraph*, 1 June) asked both Conservative Party members and voters who they would like to succeed Howard. At this stage, David Davis was the clear favourite, as Table 6.2 reveals.

	Conservative members (%)	Conservative voters (%)
David Davis	54	36
David Cameron	30	15
Liam Fox	24	16
Ken Clarke	19	23
Malcolm Rifkind	13	9

Source: YouGov, June 2005.

Table 6.2 Who should be the next Tory leader?

By the end of August, though, Clarke's swashbuckling entry into the contest had made it seem more open — as Table 6.3 reveals:

	Conservative members (%)	Conservative voters (%)
David Davis	30	17
Ken Clarke	30	34
David Cameron	16	7
Liam Fox	13	8
Malcolm Rifkind	4	3

Source: YouGov, September 2005

Table 6.3 Who should be the next Tory leader?

This same poll also found that, among all voters, Clarke topped the poll with 28%, leading Davis by 19% and Cameron by 25%. Among party members, Clarke was also thought to have the best chance of winning the next general election (43% to Davis's 27% and Cameron's 10%). However, 25% of party members said they would 'seriously consider leaving the party' if Clarke became leader, a much higher figure than that applying to a Davis or Cameron leadership. In short, Clarke was the most popular candidate — but also the most divisive.

As the Tory conference approached, it seemed the leadership campaign would hinge on whether Clarke could (a) get beyond the parliamentary stages of the contest and thus appeal to the membership, and (b) allay the hostility to him among Eurosceptic activists. If Clarke failed to meet these challenges, it was assumed the leadership would fall to Davis. But this conjecture failed to foresee some remarkable developments.

Why was the 2005 Tory conference so important?

Commentators have often portrayed the Tory conference as a risible affair — a jamboree of blue-rinse, right-wing ladies having little or no impact on serious politics. This analysis was always unfair and overlooked the influence of the 1963 Tory conference in determining the successor to Harold Macmillan. The power of this underrated event was to surface dramatically in 2005.

Although the conference agenda contained the usual bland motions and debates, it was wholly overshadowed by an *X Factor*-like contest involving the five leadership candidates. Each of them had the chance to make a 15 minute, set-piece speech, establishing their vision for the party and their credentials as a future PM. Few imagined these speeches would have such an effect upon the course of the contest.

Rifkind

Sir Malcolm's speech came first, and it underlined his reputation as a fluent, witty orator, deploying his training as a QC to splendid effect. However, according to *Newsnight*'s straw polls (taken at the conference), it did little to raise Rifkind's support as a future leader.

Clarke

Clarke's oration the next day was a typically knockabout affair, aimed to show that he alone had the experience and robustness to damage Gordon Brown at the next general election. By the end, he seemed to have justified the view that the final, all-party contest should be a Davis–Clarke battle.

Cameron

This assumption was shaken the following day by a speech from the self-styled 'young pretender', David Cameron. In an emotive speech redolent of Blair circa 1994, Cameron spoke of compassionate, middle-of-the-road conservatism, and wowed delegates with a speech low on substance but high on charm and charisma. By the end, his profile within the party had risen dramatically — and his speech was almost certainly the main reason for his eventual victory 2 months later.

Davis

The shadow home secretary's speech did mortal damage to his prospects of leading the party. Among delegates, it confirmed his shortcomings as a platform speaker and was almost devoid of wit and sparkle — a painful contrast to Cameron's *tour de force* of the previous day. It seemed too focused on his home affairs brief, and made no effort to offer some overarching vision. As one delegate told a reporter: 'if he can't inspire us, what chance of him inspiring the country?'

Fox

Liam Fox's speech was mainly pitched at the 'unreconstructed' wing of the party. As such, it stressed the record of the Thatcher governments and traditional moral values. It was a competent and well-delivered piece that signalled Fox's emergence as leader of the party's right.

The 2005 Tory conference gave Cameron's campaign unstoppable momentum and fatally wounded Davis's. Cameron's speech was also a blow to Clarke, as he was no longer seen as the main centre-left alternative to Davis, or as possessing a unique capacity to attract Liberal Democrat supporters.

A YouGov poll of activists, taken shortly after the conference, shows that its effect was profound.

Cameron	35%
Clarke	24%
Davis	21%
Fox	20%

Source: YouGov, October 2005

Table 6.4 Who should be the next Tory leader?

The parliamentary ballots: democracy denied?

With the conference over, the contest moved on to its more decisive stages, with ballots designed to eliminate one candidate at a time. The process was simplified slightly by Rifkind's withdrawal just after the conference.

In the run up to the first ballot, the key issue was who would come third — Clarke or Fox — and thus avoid elimination. With Davis's support among activists falling, Clarke's backers argued that if their man could come third, then in the second ballot he could leapfrog Davis into second place; with Davis's campaign 'holed' by his conference performance, only Clarke now had the ability to defeat Cameron. However, the prospect of a Clarke–Cameron contest was not appealing to right-wing MPs (notably the Cornerstone Group), who became increasingly attracted to Fox. This was duly confirmed in the result of the first ballot on 18 October.

Davis	62
Cameron	56
Fox	42
Clarke	38

Clarke eliminated

Table 6.5 First ballot of Tory MPs

Apart from ending forever Clarke's leadership ambitions, the result also confirmed the limitations of the existing system. Ordinary party members only have a choice of two candidates. Yet, according to Table 6.4, their second most popular candidate would not be available to them, having been ejected by MPs.

The other message from the first ballot was that Davis had lost support among MPs since the start of the campaign, when his team claimed 'guaranteed' support from at least 66 MPs. Indeed, at one stage they had boasted he could even win support from a majority of MPs and thus end the contest there and then. By contrast, Cameron's support continued to improve, despite tabloid insinuations about his having taken drugs as a student. Cameron's rise was confirmed by the second ballot 2 days later.

Cameron	90
Davis	57
Fox	51

Fox eliminated

Table 6.6 Second ballot of Tory MPs

In some ways, the result was a relief for Davis: it had been suggested that Fox alone had the credibility to challenge Cameron among the members and that Davis could therefore slip from first to third place (just as Michael Portillo did in the 2001 contest). However, although Davis survived, he had to face a number of uncomfortable facts:

- There was a further slippage of support among MPs after the first ballot (see the box below).
- There was no evidence that he had attracted new backers.
- He was no longer the preferred choice of the party at Westminster. This weakness had crippled Iain Duncan Smith during his ill-starred leadership — as most party members were all too aware.

Although the ballots were secret, enough MPs were open about their voting for the *Daily Telegraph* to conduct a survey. It is clear that, in the second ballot, the bulk of Clarke's supporters switched to Cameron as the new champion of one-nation conservatism. The information is shown in the box below.

Who backed whom?

The information relates to voting in the second ballot. Where MPs are known to have voted differently in the first ballot, the candidate they backed previously is included in brackets after their names.

Cameron: Peter Ainsworth, Michael Ancram, James Arbuthnot (Clarke), Tony Baldry, Greg Barker, Richard Benyon, John Bercow (Clarke), John Butterfill, Douglas Carswell, David Curry (Clarke), Stephen Dorrell (Clarke), Nadine Dorries (Davis), James Duddridge (Davis), Alan Duncan, Philip Dunne, Tobias Ellwood, Edward Garnier (Clarke), Nick Gibb, Michael Gove, James Gray, John Greenway (Clarke), John Gummer (Clarke), David Heathcoat-Amory (Fox), Charles Hendry (Clarke), Adam Holloway (Davis), John Horam (Clarke), Jeremy Hunt, Nick Hurd, Michael Jack, Stewart Jackson (Davis), Bernard Jenkin, Boris Johnson, Robert Key, Jacqui Lait, Mark Lancaster, Andrew Lansley (Clarke), Oliver Letwin,

Peter Lilley, Peter Luff, John Maples (Davis), Michael Mates (Clarke), Theresa May, Maria Miller, Anne Milton, David Mundell, Andrew Murrison (Davis), George Osborne, Andrew Pelling (Clarke), Malcolm Rifkind (Clarke), Andrew Robathan, Hugh Robertson, Grant Shapps, Nicholas Soames, John Stanley, Anthony Steen (Clarke), Graham Stuart, Hugo Swire, David Tredinnick, Ed Vaizey, Peter Viggers, Theresa Villiers, Ben Wallace (Davis), Rob Wilson, Jeremy Wright, George Young (Clarke).

Davis: Richard Bacon, John Baron, Graham Brady, Julian Brazier, James Brokenshire, Greg Clark, Derek Conway, David Davies, Philip Davies, Quentin Davies, Jonathan Djanogly, Nigel Evans, David Evennett, Michael Falon, Mark Field, Eric Forth, Roger Gale, David Gauke, Paul Goodman, Damian Green, Dominic Grieve, Philip Hammond, Nick Herbert, Mark Hoban, Philip Hollobone, David Jones, Julie Kirkbride, Greg Knight, David Lidington, Tim Loughton, Andrew Mackay, Anne Main, Humphrey Malins, Patrick Mercer, Andrew Mitchell, Malcolm Moss, Richard Ottoway, James Paice, Mike Penning, Eric Pickles, Mark Pritchard, David Ruffley, Lee Scott, Keith Simpson, Richard Spring, Robert Syms, Ian Taylor, Shailesh Vara, Charles Walker, Bill Wiggin, David Willets, David Wilshire.

Fox: David Burrows, Geoffrey Cox, Stephen Crabb, Mark Francois, Robert Goodwill, Chris Grayling, Justine Greening, Stephen Hammond, Greg Hands, Mark Harper, John Hayes, Oliver Heald, Gerald Howarth, Daniel Kawczynski, Eleanor Laing, Brooks Newmark, Stephen O'Brien, Owen Paterson, John Redwood, Laurence Robertson, Gary Streeter, Desmond Swayne, Nigel Waterson (Clarke), Angela Watkinson, John Whittingdale, Ann Widdecombe (Clarke).

Undeclared: Adam Afriyie, David Amess (Davis), Peter Atkinson, Henry Bellingham, Paul Beresford (Davis), Brian Binley, Crispin Blunt, Peter Bone, Tim Boswell, Peter Bottomley, Angela Browning, Simon Burns, Alastair Burt (Clarke), Bill Cash, Chris Chope, James Clappison (Clarke), Ken Clarke (Clarke), Geoffrey Clifton-Brown, Patrick Cormack, Iain Duncan Smith, Michael Fabricant, Christopher Fraser (Fox), Cheryl Gillan (Davis), William Hague, Alan Haselhurst, Douglas Hogg, Michael Howard, Edward Leigh, Julian Lewis, Ian Liddell-Grainger (Davis), Michael Lord, David Maclean, Francis Maude, Anne McIntosh, Patrick McLoughlin, John Penrose (Clarke), Mark Prisk, John Randall, Andrew Rosindell, Andrew Selous, Richard Shepherd, Mark Simmonds (Davis), Caroline Spelman, Michael Spicer, Bob Spink, Peter Tapsell, Andrew Turner (Fox), Andrew Tyrie (Clarke), Robert Walter (Clarke), Ann Winterton (Davis), Nicholas Winteron (Davis), Tim Yeo (Clarke).

Beyond parliament: did the campaign make a difference?

The parliamentary rounds cleared, Davis and Cameron embarked upon a 6-week campaign to win the support of constituency party members. There were times when it looked less like a campaign than a coronation for Cameron. A YouGov poll at the end of October (based on a survey of 1,000 grass-root Tories) showed that Cameron had a lead of over 30%, while over half the party's MPs had declared their support for him by 12 November — Liam Fox, Tim Yeo, Bill Cash and William Hague being among those who came off the fence. According to many grass-root officials, this clear backing from the parliamentary party was 'bound to influence' the extra-parliamentary electorate.

However, there were MPs who tried to persuade their associations to ignore the parliamentary mood. Graham Brady (Altrincham and Sale West) wrote a lengthy letter to his constituency members in support of Davis, claiming that Cameron was 'apparently indifferent' to the fate of grammar schools — a thorny issue in one of the few areas where they survive. But a poll for the *Sale and Altrincham Messenger* found that most activists chose to ignore their MP's advice, sensing it was unrepresentative of MPs generally.

In the course of the campaign, the candidates addressed 11 hustings of party members across the country, as well as partaking in head-to-head debates on television programmes like *Question Time* and radio shows like *Woman's Hour*. It was unclear how much impact these events had. The 253,689 ballot papers were sent out on 4 November and, according to many constituency officials, the bulk of recipients returned them 'within days' (*Sunday Telegraph*, 13 November). In short, the crucial moments in the battle for the Tory leadership came not during the all-party campaign but at the party conference and in the parliamentary ballots that followed.

What divided the candidates?

One-nation vs Thatcherite conservatism?
For many in the media, this was a straightforward left–right battle for the soul of conservatism. On the one hand, we had the supposedly Thatcherite Davis, whose council-house background echoed the humble origins of the Lady herself, and who emphasised the classic Thatcherite mix of tax cuts and robust law and order. On the other hand, we had the one-nation, Old Etonian Cameron, whose patrician concerns about 'the social fabric' echoed that of pre-1960s Tory leaders.

Style vs substance?
For Davis supporters, the contest was also a clash of substance over style — or, as one wag put it (alluding to rumours about Cameron's student days), 'substance vs substances'. Davis unveiled economic policies that involved cutting public spending by 4% of GDP so as to allow £38 billion worth of tax cuts (the 2005 Tory manifesto promised no more than £4 billion). Cameron, by contrast, seemed 'policy lite', and warned against making detailed promises years before the next election. Instead, he preferred the 'big picture', commending a 'new Conservative vision' that would link individual choice to social responsibility. In his claims that Tories should 'reach out' and be 'less stuffy', there were echoes of Michael Portillo's 'metro-Conservatism', lately

articulated by George Osborne and other 'Notting Hill Tories'. However, unlike Portillo, Cameron supported the return of a marriage tax allowance and measures that upheld the 'traditional family unit' — a view which helped secure support from the socially authoritarian Cornerstone Group of MPs.

A clash of style?

Despite its professed contempt for 'image', the Davis team was not uninterested in stylistic considerations. Davis was consistently marketed as the 'gritty' outsider, more attuned to society's have-nots and better placed to win back the north (Davis was born in Yorkshire and his seat is there). In contrast to Cameron, Davis was paraded as a man of solid experience — 13 years in industry before serving in Major's government — and the perfect antidote to New Labour spin and frothy presentation.

Cameron, meanwhile, almost gloried in the comparisons with Tony Blair 10 years earlier, happy to highlight both his youth and young family, while promising a 'fresh' and 'up-to-the-minute' path for his party. It was interesting that he saw no need to play down his privileged background (a factor which dogged Douglas Hurd's leadership bid in 1990), and the party seemed unfazed about electing its first Etonian leader since 1965.

A consensual election?

Despite the areas of difference listed above, it must be remembered that there was a huge amount of common ground between the two candidates, as the comparisons below reveal.

Davis and Cameron: their final policy agendas

Tax and spending: Cameron wanted to divide the 'proceeds of growth' between tax cuts and increased spending, but hinted that the improvement of public services would be the priority. Davis promised a 'low tax, free market economy' where state spending as a percentage of GDP would fall to pre-Blair levels.

Health: Cameron said that NHS services should be provided either by the NHS itself or independent operators (not dissimilar to Blair's position). Davis agreed, stressing the need to give foundation hospitals much more autonomy.

Education: Both candidates backed the government's plan to 'free' state schools from central and local government management; Davis also stressed the need for schools to offer even more vocational training.

Law and order: Both wanted to amend the Human Rights Act so that the UK could deport terror suspects; Davis also recommended more prisons and locally elected police officers.

Europe: Both candidates called for the repatriation of certain powers from the EU, along with its enlargement.

Family: Cameron called for the restoration of the marriage tax allowance; Davis's support for 'family-friendly tax structures' was less specific.

Iraq: Both supported the war.

Constitution: Cameron called for more elective mayors and an elected House of Lords; Davis more vaguely supported 'decentralisation of power'.

Party organisation: Cameron argued that the Tories should 'look and feel and talk like a completely different organisation', and, like Davis, called for more female and ethnic minority candidates. Davis called for more localised campaigning and the 'democratisation' of policy discussion.

The result

The longest Conservative leadership contest ever ended on 5 December, with the announcement of the result. Few were surprised that Cameron won, though many were taken aback by the scale of his victory. The figures are also revealing in that they point to a shrinking Conservative membership. In the less well-reported, and arguably less interesting, leadership contest of 2001, 256,000 party members registered a vote. Significantly fewer did so in 2005, indicating the party has lost a fifth of its members in the last 4 years alone.

David Cameron	134,446 (67%)
David Davis	64,398 (32%)
Ballot papers returned	198,844 (78%)

Table 6.7 The final result

Why did Cameron win?

A YouGov poll, conducted among party voters just before the final result, makes for interesting reading (see Table 6.8). It shows that members did recognise Cameron's inexperience and his rather superficial approach to policy. Had the party been looking for 'substance', 'experience', 'ballast' and 'heavyweight' leadership — as it once always did — it seems clear that Davis would have won. Indeed, this was why Davis was tipped to win easily when the race started just after the general election.

Instead, it seems that the party fell in love with David Cameron after his performance at the Tory conference and, as is often the case with the love-struck, became indifferent to his faults. The poll shows clearly that Cameron won almost wholly on the basis of cosmetic criteria, such as his television image, relative youth and boundless self-confidence.

These reasons for Cameron's victory are not dissimilar to those behind Blair's in the Labour leadership contest of 1994. But it should be remembered that Blair and a few allies effectively reinvented Labour between 1994 and 1997, and were anything but inclusive in their management of the party. As one veteran of the period remarked, 'we voted for a rough voyage to new shores — and we got one'.

By contrast, Cameron promises to be less cliquish in relation to the rest of the party and rebuffs any notion that he and his 'Notting Hill' allies are a vanguard, set to hijack the party. Throughout his leadership campaign, Cameron promised a 'shadow cabinet of all the talents' and played down the idea that the party would be 'starting over' — hence the endorsement of Tory grandees like Lords Hurd, Heseltine and Patten. This helped to reassure the party's more nervous elements.

Furthermore, Cameron's Etonian background led some to speculate that the party was returning to its patrician, semi-aristocratic character after an interregnum of 40 years. As one MP told the *New Statesman*, 'we've had enough of these prickly meritocrats and Davis was just too reminiscent of Heath. It's time to be led again by people of quality who don't have chips on their shoulders'. This prompts the wider point that the UK has got over its infatuation with 'classlessness' — a legacy of the 1960s — and is again at ease with inherited wealth and opportunity.

With which candidate do you associate the following statements?	Cameron	Davis
He comes over well on television.	71%	17%
He would appeal to those who didn't vote Tory in 2005.	64%	21%
He comes over as a man of the future.	68%	9%
If he were leader, the party could make a fresh start.	59%	12%
He is better placed to lead a united party.	59%	27%
He would be a more formidable opponent of Blair/Brown.	50%	35%
He is bold and willing to take risks.	45%	20%
He looks like a potential PM.	49%	19%
He has lots of self-confidence.	44%	9%
He lacks political experience.	60%	2%
He has style but not much substance.	42%	7%
He seems a lightweight.	28%	11%
He has well-developed views on policy.	13%	50%

Source: YouGov, 1 December.

Table 6.8 Why did Cameron win? The views of Tory members

Summary

What are the implications of Cameron's victory?

■ *'Compassionate', 'reach out' conservatism is in vogue.* Davis's heavy defeat marks the end of 'core vote' conservatism and the belief that the party can win from a clear right-wing position. Cameron, unlike Hague in 2001 and Howard in 2005, will make a clear pitch for the middle ground at the next election and consciously try to squeeze the Liberal Democrats. In short, the Tories may have finally escaped the shadow of Margaret Thatcher.

- *The importance of the Tory conference was confirmed.* An event often dismissed by journalists, the 2005 Tory conference showed how vital an occasion it can be, giving impetus to the campaign of David Cameron and breaking that of David Davis. At a time when party members are less deferential than ever, a party's main gathering should never be treated lightly — and the fate of Davis is a warning to MPs who think otherwise.

- *The nature of political campaigning has altered.* In the course of the campaign beyond Westminster, the two candidates engaged in a number of television and radio debates with each other, making it (according to Andrew Marr) 'the most open and accessible leadership campaign ever conducted'. This type of head-to-head campaigning, a long-time feature of US presidential elections, could now prove impossible to resist at general elections — whatever the wishes of Gordon Brown. In other words, by establishing such a clear precedent, the Tory contest in 2005 may have altered irreversibly the nature of UK election campaigns and the role of the electronic media.

- *Howard's attempt at rule change had fateful results.* It meant, quite simply, that no new leader could be found until after the Tory conference. Had Howard simply resigned in May — and not committed himself to a rules debate beforehand — it is likely that David Davis would have been elected new leader by the end of August. Howard's decision is made even more poignant by the failure of any new rules to emerge. Upon such strange twists does the course of politics often depend.

- *Conservatives are being taken seriously again.* Some commentators now argue that the 'stardust' that surrounded Blair 10 years ago now surrounds Cameron, and that New Labour looks as jaded and sleazy as the Tories did in the mid 1990s. Cameron's recruitment of Hague to his shadow cabinet also suggests that the Tories have regained their thirst for power. For the first time since the 1980s, momentum could be with the Conservative Party.

Chapter 7

The Conservatives: a blue tomorrow?

About this chapter

On the night of the 2005 election, there was mild celebration inside Conservative Central Office — a clear sense that a corner had been turned. Yet the party's overall performance was still dismal. This chapter will answer the following questions:

- How did the party perform in 2005?
- Should the Tories be optimistic or pessimistic?
- Will the Tories return to power in the foreseeable future?

6 May 2005: reasons to be cheerful?

Reading some of the newspapers the day after the 2005 general election, and listening to some of the comments made by senior Conservatives, one would have been forgiven for thinking we had a new Conservative government.

Tory elation, 6 May 2005

'TORIES GIVE BLAIR A BLOODY NOSE' (*Daily Mail*)

'RETURN OF THE TORIES' (*Daily Express*)

'Overall, a very good night for us' (Michael Ancram, shadow foreign secretary)

'We're the ones who are smiling tonight!' (Sir Malcolm Rifkind)

'The dark days are behind us…the Conservatives are back!' (Liam Fox, party chair)

Before exposing the absurdity of such claims, we need to try to understand them. Why did some Tories feel they had cause for modest satisfaction after the 2005 general election?

Progress in seats?

In 2005 the Tories made a net gain of 35 seats — the first time the party had gained any seats since the general election of 1983.

- *The Tories gained seats from Labour* (see the box below). The seats the party took from Labour in Greater London — notably Putney and Enfield Southgate (Michael Portillo's old constituency) — had totemic value, suggesting the party was again appealing to more sophisticated, metropolitan voters.

- *The Tories gained seats from the Lib Dems* (see the box below). This also had symbolic importance, for two reasons: first, it suggested that anti-Labour, middle-class voters, having flirted with the third party, were now 'returning to the fold'; second, it suggested that the Tories were reaffirming themselves as the principal opposition to Labour. This was underlined by the fact that...
- *The Tories widened their seat lead over the Lib Dems*. This rose from 114 in 2001 to 131 in 2005. Many Tories felt they had avoided a 'nightmare scenario' in which the party were pushed into third place by the Liberal Democrats — a scenario that looked quite likely during Iain Duncan Smith's leadership (2001–03).
- *The Tories avoided 'celtic meltdown'*. The phrase was coined in 1997 after the party failed to win a single seat in either Wales or Scotland. In 2005, however, the Tories gained one seat in Scotland (though losing the seat they gained in 2001) and gained three seats in Wales — the first time the party had gained in Wales since 1983.
- *'One more heave' could destroy Labour's majority*. Should the Tories repeat their 2005 rate of progress at the next election, Labour will probably lose its majority: only 33 seats stand between Labour and a hung parliament. And the Tories are in second place in 27 of those constituencies.

Tory gains, 2005
From Labour:

Bexleyheath and Crawford	Monmouth
Braintree	Northampton South
Clwyd West	Peterborough
Croydon Central	Preseli Pembrokeshire
Dumfriesshire, Clydesdale and Tweedale	Putney
Enfield Southgate	Reading East
Forest of Dean	Rugby and Kenilworth
Gravesham	Scarborough and Witney
Hammersmith and Fulham	Shipley
Harwich	Shrewsbury and Atcham
Hemel Hempstead	St Albans
Hornchurch	Wellingborough
Ilford North	Welwyn Hatfield
Kettering	Wimbledon
Lancaster and Wyre	Wrekin
Milton Keynes North East	Total: 31

From the Liberal Democrats:
Guildford
Ludlow
Newbury
Torridge and West Devon
Weston-super-Mare
Total: 5

Progress in votes?

- *Vote haemorrhage stemmed*. Having seen their total vote shrink at the previous two elections, in 2005 the Tories added to their total number of supporters.
- *Vote gap with Labour narrowed*. The Tory vote share is now only 3% smaller than Labour's, compared with 12% in 1997 and 10% in 2001.
- *Southern comfort*. In many London and southern constituencies, there were significantly large swings in favour of the Conservatives (their vote share went up by as much as 15.5% in Brentwood and Ongar); this reinforced the point made above about their 'recapture' of metropolitan voters and core supporters. Among southern voters generally (outside London), the Conservatives won 42% of votes, compared to 23% for Labour and 29% for the Liberal Democrats (see Table 7.1).
- *Most popular party in England*. Even though they won 97 seats fewer than Labour, the Tories won 0.2% more support from voters in England.

Region	Votes (%)	Position	Lead over second party/distance behind first party (% of votes)	Seats
England	35.7	1	+0.2	193
Scotland	15.8	4	−20.1	1
Wales	21.4	2	−21.3	3
Northwest England	28.7	2	−16.5	9
Northeast England	19.5	3	−32.5	1
Yorkshire and Humberside	29.1	2	−14.5	9
Southeast England	45	1	+19.6	58
Southwest England	38.6	1	+6	22
London	31.9	2	−7	21
Eastern England	43.3	1	+13.5	40
East Midlands	37.1	2	−1.9	18
West Midlands	34.8	2	−4.1	15
UK	32.3	2	−2.9	197

Table 7.1 Conservative Party support in the UK regions

Why some progress?

It seems fair to conclude that the Tories were less unsuccessful in 2005 than they were in 1997 or 2001. There are several factors that explain the party's (albeit modest) revival.

- *Disillusionment with Labour*. Issues like Iraq, tuition fees and Blunkett-type scandals had all conspired to dent voters' faith in the government. Even so, there was no assurance that such disenchantment would benefit the Tories: by 2005, there were a number of high-profile opposition parties trying to exploit Labour's unpopularity. To understand why these parties did not eclipse the Conservatives, we have to look at other factors behind the Tories' gains.

- *Less divided party*. Largely because Europe had been sidelined as an issue, voters perceived the Tories to be more united than at any time since 1992.
- *More competent Tory leadership*. Although voters did not warm to Michael Howard, there was evidence that they held him in more respect than his two predecessors (see Table 7.2). This seemed deserved: unlike William Hague and IDS, Howard had top-flight cabinet experience and brought much more discipline to the party machine.

Gallup 2001:	
Would William Hague make a good prime minister?	Yes: 18%
YouGov 2003:	
Would Iain Duncan Smith make a good prime minister?	Yes: 15%
YouGov 2005:	
Would Michael Howard make a good prime minister?	Yes: 25%

Table 7.2 Popularity of Tory leaders

- *Supremacy on certain key issues*. On the issues of law and order (ranked third among voters' concerns) and immigration (ranked fifth), voters appeared to trust the Tories more than Labour (see Table 7.3). For this, credit must again be given to the leadership, which promoted these issues ruthlessly during the 6 months leading up to the election.

Question: With which party do you associate the following statements?	
They have the best policies on law and order.	
Conservatives: 31%	Labour: 30%
They have the best policies on immigration.	
Conservatives: 35%	Labour: 24%

Table 7.3 Tory supremacy on key issues

- *A tighter campaign*. Following the Tories' shapeless campaigns of 1997 and 2001, it was generally agreed that the party's senior organiser — Lynton Crosby — brought polish and professionalism to their campaign in 2005. This involved greater use of information technology — notably the 'Votervault' computer system used by the Republicans in the USA 6 months earlier — plus advice obtained by Crosby from Karl Rove, the US campaign strategist who masterminded President Bush's victories of 2000 and 2004.
- *'Tactical unwind'*. In both the 1997 and 2001 general elections, the Tories lost up to 50 seats owing to tactical voting by centre-left voters. But in the 2005 election, Lib Dem supporters were much less willing to switch their support to Labour in seats where Labour was the main opposition to the Tories. As such, tactical voting receded (a phenomenon described by John Curtice as 'tactical unwind'), leading to a fragmentation of centre-left support and the Tories regaining a number of seats — even though their own support scarcely improved from 2001. An example is given in Table 7.4.

	2001	2005
Labour	**22,253** (elected)	17,152
Conservatives	18,815	**18,960** (elected)
Lib Dems	6,173	11,487

Table 7.4 The demise of tactical voting in 2005: Shrewsbury and Atcham

Another shameful failure?

Despite the initial elation of some Conservatives, it soon became clear that the 2005 general election was another abject failure for the party, with a Conservative government still looking far off.

The party's total vote rose by less than half a million from 2001: as a result, the Conservative vote of 8.7 million was its second lowest since 1945 — lower even than in 1997, when the party crashed to what many thought was rock bottom. The Conservatives' vote share is flatlining: it rose by just 0.6%, to 32.3% of the UK vote, which meant that — for the third successive general election — the party failed to win even a third of the votes.

The party's share of seats is still low. For the third election in a row, it failed to win even 200 seats. Apart from 1997 and 2001, the Tory tally of 197 seats is its worst since 1906. It is worth recalling that the Tories still have fewer seats than Labour achieved at its low-point election of 1983 — an election from which Labour took 14 years to recover.

The Conservative Party still looks like an England-only party. Just 2% of its seats are in Scotland and Wales. Even in the north of England, the party made no progress: there are still no Tory MPs in Manchester, Liverpool, Leeds, Sheffield or Newcastle; in all these cities they were out-polled by the Lib Dems (see the box below). The party also failed to win most of the key northern marginals (e.g. Cheadle), while the party's share of the vote went down in the northeast, northwest, Yorkshire and Humberside, and the Midlands. In some seats, its share of the vote fell sharply — for example, by 10% in Burnley.

The Lib Dems obstructed a serious Tory recovery. This was for two reasons. First, even though the Tories made some progress nationally, they still lost three seats to the Lib Dems (Solihull, Taunton and Westmorland and Lonsdale). Second, it was the Lib Dems, not the Tories, who were the main beneficiaries of Labour's decline: about seven out of every eight Labour 'switchers' went to the Lib Dems, who have replaced the Tories as the main opposition to Labour in many northern constituencies.

Finally, the Tories made no progress with middle-class or women voters: indeed, the party's vote share fell within these two groups. Among middle-class women voters aged 25–54, the party's vote share fell by 4%. In view of the fact that middle-class voters outnumber working class voters, and that women voters outnumber men, this stands as a crucial failure.

Some 'killer facts' for the Tories

After the 2005 election, the Tories have:

- 1/62 seats in Scotland
- 3/39 seats in Wales
- 1/28 seats in Greater Manchester
- not even second place in a single Manchester or Liverpool constituency
- 1/38 seats in West and South Yorkshire
- 0/16 seats in Merseyside

Why did the Tories fail again?

- *Not trusted on key issues*. On three of the four issues ranked most important by voters — health (first), education (second) and economic management (fourth) — the Tories were seen as less competent and trustworthy than Labour by voters.
- *Failure of 'core vote' strategy*. The party's failure to outperform Labour on the key issues points to the failure of Lynton Crosby's 'dog whistle' strategy. This was designed to highlight those issues on which the Tories were traditionally strong (law and order, immigration) and then 'whistle in' the party's natural supporters. In the event, this strategy seemed only to alienate a new swathe of floating voters.
- *Howard was not popular with voters*. The 2005 Tory campaign was perhaps the most presidential it has ever fought, dominated by the presence of Michael Howard. His expulsion from the party of Howard Flight, the shadow minister who implied that the Tories' tax-cut policy could be bolder, was designed to show the leader's iron grip on the party. But there was a huge problem with this approach. Although voters generally saw Howard as a better Tory leader than his two predecessors, only 31% thought him an 'asset to his party', compared to the 52% who considered him a liability (YouGov, April 2005). And, though 67% of voters 'did not trust' Blair, fewer than a quarter thought Howard would make a better PM.
- *A lack of active constituency campaigners*. One of the reasons why the Tory campaign had to be so presidential was that the party had weak organisation at grass-root level. For several years now, it has lacked active constituency volunteers, able to put the Tory message into a local context. With voter dealignment, and the disappearance of uniform voting patterns, these volunteers seem more important than ever — but they are scarce among an elderly Tory membership.
- *Problems with the Tory 'brand'*. There was evidence that the party still has a serious image problem, dating from the failings of the last Conservative government (see Table 7.5).
- *Still no clear raison d'être*. Underpinning the Tories' problems might be a failure to clarify what they're actually for now that socialism and

communism have been effectively defeated. The clear objectives that drove the Thatcher governments (like the assault on trade union power and nationalised industries) are no longer present, and the party is yet to find an overriding purpose in the Blair era.

Question: With which party do you associate the following statements?
It seems to appeal to one section of society rather than the whole country.
Conservatives: 48%   Labour: 20%
It seems stuck in the past.
Conservatives: 45%   Labour: 11%
It seems old and tired.
Conservatives: 44%   Labour: 18%
Question: Do you agree with the following statement?
I still hold against the Conservatives their record in government under John Major.
Agree: 56%

Source: YouGov

Table 7.5 Negative perceptions of the Tory Party, 2005

A blue tomorrow?

What are the Conservative Party's prospects? Is there a realistic chance of it returning to power in the foreseeable future?

The pessimists' view

Many commentators, like the *Guardian's* Michael White, believe the Tories face an 'electoral Everest' which is impossible to climb. Certainly, there are a number of daunting factors that the party must confront:

- *The party needs to win a further 126 seats to gain a majority.* In other words, the Tories will have to gain almost four times as many seats as they did in 2005.
- *In many target seats, the Lib Dems are 'in the way'.* In former Tory marginals such as Edinburgh South, Watford, Oxford East and Aberdeen South, the Tories have been pushed into third place by the Lib Dems — thus making it even harder for these vital seats to be regained. That the Tories failed to regain Cheadle in the by-election of July 2005 — a seat they held with a majority of 16,000 in 1992 — was further proof that they are no longer the natural party of middle class, suburban voters.
- *The Tories need a record swing in their favour to gain power.* To date, the highest pro-Tory swing ever achieved at a general election was 5% (in 1979). For the Tories to gain a majority at the next election, they will need a swing of roughly 9%. In 2005, such a swing was only achieved in three constituencies.
- *The Tories are disadvantaged by the electoral system.* Because Labour seats have fewer voters, it is estimated that Labour could still win a majority of seats even if it polled 3% fewer votes than the Tories. By contrast, the Tories may need 10% more votes than Labour to achieve the barest of Commons majorities.

- *The Tories are uncertain of their future direction.* The 'grand debate' inside the party, launched after the 2005 election, has only revealed how unsure the party is about where to go next — liberal modernisers like Tim Yeo oppose the more authoritarian ideas of people like David Davis. This problem is compounded by polls that show differences between the views of party members and those of Conservative voters (see Table 7.6).
- *A redundant ideology?* Scholars like John Gray suggest that the Conservative Party is in terminal decline because conservatism as an ideology is now irrelevant. It emerged after 1789 to combat the birth of egalitarianism, and some argue that it started to decay after 1989, with the end of the Cold War and the subsequent demise of socialism and communism. In other words, the removal of conservatism's main enemies has removed the need for conservatism. The success of New Labour — a party that has stolen the traditional Tory theme of private enterprise plus a concern for the social fabric — has only underlined the question: what is the Conservative Party *for*?

Should the Conservative Party...	Tory members agreeing (%)	Tory voters agreeing (%)
Extend privatisation and reduce the size of the state?	65	41
Promise big tax cuts?	48	34
Replace council tax with local income tax?	41	60
Promise to halt immigration?	35	51
Make public services more efficient but not radically reform them?	32	53

Source: *Daily Telegraph*, 8 June 2005.

Table 7.6 Conflict between Tory members and Tory voters

The optimists' view

On the other hand, the Conservative Party has suffered crises before (in both 1846 and 1906 it practically fell apart) and still recovered. Inside the party, there are those who think that its ancient versatility — and determination to govern — will again come to the rescue. They make the following points to support their case:

- *The 2005 defeat was a wake-up call.* Once the initial (and absurd) euphoria of gaining 33 seats had subsided, most Conservative MPs accepted that the party had now suffered three emphatic election defeats and could no longer 'chug along' hoping for better days. In other words, radical reform was now needed and Howard's launch of the 'grand debate' has made such reform more likely. It remains to be seen whether the party will find the right prescription. But at least it now appreciates the scale of its problems.
- *There are gaps in the political market.* Tory modernisers (like party chair Francis Maude) argue that politics needs a party that combines economic liberalism with social liberalism; a belief in the free market plus a clear acceptance of social diversity and alternative lifestyles. Were Conservatives

to adopt this quasi-libertarian combination, they might have a programme that is distinctive, modern and — for Conservatives — refreshingly upbeat. The chances of adopting such a programme have been enhanced by 'the class of 2005', as discussed below.

- *The parliamentary party has been infused with new talent.* It is widely agreed that the party's newly elected MPs have brought vigour, modernity, diversity and talent to the party at Westminster (see the box below). Likewise, young Tories elected in 2001, like George Osborne and David Cameron, have been propelled to front-bench status since 2005. As the influence of these younger Tories grows, so might the party's chances of reconnecting with voters.

- *Other parties also have problems.* Since winning in 2001, Labour has been beset by divisions, and Blair's imminent resignation might only highlight the tensions between New and Old Labour. Having not done as well as expected in the general election, the Lib Dems have also shown signs of disunity, with a growing divide between supporters of Charles Kennedy, who think the party should stick with the centre-left policies it espoused in 2005, and the party's free marketeers (like Mark Oaten and David Laws), who favour a more centre-right position. These intra-party differences could reap rewards for the Conservatives.

- *The Tories could be revived by a new leader.* The advent of David Cameron as party leader — youthful, untainted by previous Tory governments and supposedly able to grant Conservatives a new idealism — could mark the start of a new era for the centre-right in the UK. It is interesting that the 'modernising' wing of the party, represented by Cameron and Osborne, has already had some sort of dialogue with the Liberal Democrats — a tactic previously unthinkable, given the Lib Dems' 'outside-left' leanings. However, the growing influence of Lib Dem modernisers like Oaten and Laws raises the distant possibility of a Lib–Con coalition. With the possibility of a hung parliament after the next general election (likely if the Tories have a modest vote lead over Labour), this fledgling political marriage could yet offer the Tories a route out of opposition.

Rising stars

Many of the Tories' young (and youngish) MPs have been cited as 'names to watch'. They include:

- Justine Greening (Putney), aged 35, ex-finance director
- Adam Afriyie (Windsor), aged 40, city banker, the first Tory MP of Afro-Caribbean descent
- Shailesh Vara (Cambridgeshire North West), aged 48, former accountant, the first Asian vice-chair of the party
- Greg Clarke (Tonbridge Wells) aged 46, former director of the Conservative Research Department
- Michael Gove (Surrey Heath) aged 40, *The Times* editorial writer

Summary

- The Tory performance in 2005 was better than in 2001 — but still poor.

- The party still has a grave problem with its public image.

- The party still suffers from a crisis of identity.

- The leadership contest of 2005 failed to provide a clear answer to the question of what the Tories are *for*.

- The party hopes that its new, youthful leader may yet provide an answer.

The cabinet: reshuffle by negotiation?

About this chapter

It is now commonplace to argue that cabinet government is dead. This chapter looks at the cabinet in 2005, answering key questions such as:

- What influenced the composition of Mr Blair's cabinet after the 2005 election victory?
- Why was where so little change in the 2005 reshuffle?
- Are there more reshuffles to come?
- How does the 2005 cabinet differ from that of 1997?
- Are some ministers moved too often and how does that affect delivery of government policy?
- Is there too much 'cronyism' in some ministerial appointments?

What factors influenced the composition of the 2005 cabinet?

The general election of 2005 resulted in a much smaller Labour majority. It followed a campaign during which the prime minister's style of leadership — the so-called 'control freakery' identified by former ministers such as the late Mo Mowlam — and his judgement, primarily over Iraq, had raised questions regarding his political future and the succession. Tony Blair had indicated that he would not be leading the Labour Party into a fourth general election and his choice of cabinet members following the party's historic third successive election victory was widely seen as an indication of how the transfer of power was likely to be handled. Many expected that Blair would take the opportunity to make sweeping changes in personnel.

Framing a cabinet

At the time of the 2001 general election, *The Economist* identified five considerations that might shape cabinet appointments:

- *Sex (gender)*: a need to balance the cabinet in terms of gender — particularly in light of the increasing numbers of women MPs in the Commons since 1997.
- *Colour (ethnicity):* a desire to reflect society by providing ethnic minority representation within cabinet.
- *Guilt:* a need to reward those who have lost out in previous reshuffles, or those who have shown loyalty.

- *Personality:* the need to appoint at least one or two individuals with genuine charisma, alongside other worthy but dry administrators.

- *Political balance:* a desire to reflect the full breadth of the parliamentary party within cabinet.

To these five criteria we might add two more:

- *Ability and experience:* cabinet members are required to be serving members of the legislature (MPs or Lords); they will normally have served an apprenticeship in the legislature, and in junior ministerial positions.

- *Willingness to serve:* the extent to which individuals are prepared to accept the posts offered.

Why didn't the 2005 reshuffle see more significant changes?

For those who had expected a major reshuffle in government personnel following the 2005 general election, the survival of so many pre-election office holders came as something of a surprise.

In cabinet, appointments appeared to be the result of pragmatism or compromise rather than leadership and vision. Resistance to David Blunkett's return at the head of a 'super-ministry' governing communities resulted in his appointment instead as secretary of state for work and pensions. Charles Clarke and John Prescott, it was said, had blocked the prime minister's original plan for Blunkett, fearing that their own ministries would be diminished. Other ministers tipped for a move, notably Alistair Darling, Ruth Kelly and Hilary Benn, remained in the positions they had held before the general election.

Problems with prime ministerial patronage

'In the midst of the reshuffle confusion was said to have been heated argument between Mr Blair and Mr Brown. It is believed that Mr Brown had wanted Ruth Kelly to switch to the Treasury as Chief Secretary. But Mr Blair was not keen and the move was also resisted by Miss Kelly.

Senior government officials said the reshuffle showed that Mr Blair was losing his ability to shape his own destiny and his team: "…when he tries to change things the plans go wrong because people resist and the last thing he wants to do is force the issue and make more enemies," said a government official.'

Source: adapted from an article by Toby Helm, *Daily Telegraph*, 9 May 2005.

A similar picture emerged in more junior government positions. In a *Daily Telegraph* article entitled 'Brown demands cabinet jobs for his people' (9 May 2005), Toby Helm reported that the chancellor had 'demanded that Tony Blair promote the chancellor's young protégés to government posts' and predicted that the newly elected MP for Normanton, Ed Balls, would be given a post as junior minister in the Treasury. Helm also tipped Balls's wife Yvette Cooper — already a minister — and another newly elected, former Brown special adviser, Ed Miliband (brother of David), for promotion through the ranks.

In the event, the appointment of junior to mid-ranking government ministers did not appear to reflect a major shift in the fortunes of Brownists or Blairites. Though the Blairite Beverley Hughes returned to office as minister of state for children, most of those tipped for a move either stayed where they were (Blairites such as Hazel Blears; Brownists such as Yvette Cooper and Tom Watson) or were overlooked, for the time being at least (Brownists Ed Balls and Ed Miliband).

What can we learn from the way in which the cabinet was selected in May 2005?

Patrick Wintour's *Guardian* article of 9 May (see the box below) delivered a damning assessment of the post-election reshuffle. Running with the headline 'Weak PM forced to negotiate changes to team', he charted the manner in which the prime minister had been forced to work around the ambitions of those in the frame for high office.

Reshuffle by negotiation

'Tony Blair has recently pointed to his continuing power of patronage to back his claim that he will maintain his authority in his third term, despite his plan to stand aside near its end.

But the prime minister began in the worst possible way in the aftermath of Thursday's election with a reshuffle that displayed weakness and ineptitude. One of his closest supporters and a veteran of many botched Blair reshuffles said yesterday it was never a good idea to have a reshuffle by negotiation — and that is what it looked like.'

Source: Patrick Wintour, *Guardian*, 9 May 2005.

What has become evident in the wake of Blair's decision not to lead the party into a fourth general election campaign is that leading figures in the Labour Party are now looking to safeguard their positions beyond the succession. As a result, the prime minister's ability to exercise his powers of patronage — particularly his ability to cajole key individuals into or out of specific

More reshuffles to come?

'Tony Blair is planning a radical drive to secure his New Labour legacy, his biographer claimed...The prime minister plans a major reshuffle — possibly before Christmas — to install leading Blairites in central positions...'

Source: Ben Russell, 'Blairites lined up for top jobs in reshuffle designed to strengthen prime minister', *Independent*, 1 September 2005.

departments — is far more limited than it once was; he simply doesn't have the leverage. This and the manner in which the Iraq gamble has backfired have given the impression of a lame-duck premiership, although some suggested that he was poised to try and regain the initiative before the end of 2005.

How much continuity was there in cabinet between 1997 and 2005?

The cabinet assembled in the wake of the 2005 general election certainly differed significantly from that which took office following Labour's victory in 1997. This is hardly surprising given the passage of time. Many of those in office in 1997 retired from political life (e.g. Jack Cunningham, Mo Mowlam), moved on (e.g. George Robertson to NATO, Donald Dewar to First Minister of Scotland) or resigned from office (e.g. Robin Cook, Clare Short). The Labour Party rules state that where the party has been in opposition, the first cabinet should be comprised largely of those who had previously been elected to the shadow cabinet. This could go some way towards accounting for the composition of the Labour cabinet in 1997 — 17 cabinet ministers had been elected to the party's shadow cabinet in July 1996.

Cabinets compared: 1997 and 2005			
1997		**2005 (May)**	
Prime minister	Tony Blair	Prime minister	Tony Blair
Deputy prime minister	John Prescott	Deputy prime minister	John Prescott
Chancellor of the exchequer	Gordon Brown	Chancellor of the exchequer	Gordon Brown
Foreign secretary	Robin Cook	Foreign secretary	✗ Jack Straw
Lord Chancellor	Lord Irvine	Constitutional affairs and Lord Chancellor	Lord Falconer
Home secretary	Jack Straw	Home secretary	Charles Clarke
Education and employment	David Blunkett	Education and skills	Ruth Kelly
Social security	Harriet Harman	Work and pensions	? David Blunkett
Trade and industry	Margaret Beckett	Trade and industry	Alan Johnson
Agriculture, food and fisheries	Jack Cunningham	Environment, food and rural affairs	Margaret Beckett
Defence	George Robertson	Defence	John Reid
Health	Frank Dobson	Health	Patricia Hewitt
Leader of the Commons	Ann Taylor	Leader of the Commons	Geoff Hoon
National heritage	Chris Smith	Culture, media and sport	Tessa Jowell
Northern Ireland	Mo Mowlam	Northern Ireland and Wales	Peter Hain
International development	Clare Short	International development	Hilary Benn
Leader of the Lords	Lord Richard	Leader of the Lords	Baroness Amos
Chancellor of the Duchy of Lancaster	David Clark	Chancellor of the Duchy of Lancaster	John Hutton

Cabinets compared: 1997 and 2005

1997		2005 (May)	
Transport	Gavin Strang	Transport and Scotland	Alistair Darling
Chief secretary to the Treasury	Alistair Darling	Chief secretary to the Treasury	Des Browne
Scotland	Donald Dewar	Minister of communities and local government	David Miliband
Wales	Ron Davies	Chief whip	Hilary Armstrong
		Minister without portfolio	Ian McCartney

What happened to the veterans of 1997?

David Blunkett's resignation on 2 November 2005 reduced to six the number of cabinet members surviving from Labour's first cabinet in 1997, although only three still held the same positions in 2005: Tony Blair, John Prescott and Gordon Brown.

The fact that even Prescott and Brown have held their positions for so long is significant. The post of deputy prime minister is a relatively recent innovation and has never carried great kudos, but Prescott's enduring presence reflects a need to maintain political balance within the cabinet more than it does his record as a minister. As Patrick Wintour noted (*Guardian*, 9 May 2005), 'it is part of the Westminster folklore that Mr Prescott is brilliant at running cabinet committees, and keeping the Brown–Blair show on the road, but is less good at running his big sprawling department'. Any move to dispense with the deputy prime minister would, however, risk a dangerous split between Blair and the Old Labour core support that Prescott embodies.

Brown's position is similarly secure. His support among backbenchers and public approval for his achievements at the Treasury make his dismissal unthinkable. In addition, Blair's willingness to encroach on the role of foreign secretary means that the only role more prestigious than that of chancellor would be prime minister. Brown is, therefore, unlikely to give up the reins at the Treasury until the premiership becomes available.

Prescott and Brown's ability to retain the same posts in cabinet between 1997 and 2005 is made all the more remarkable by the regularity of changes in personnel elsewhere. It is often said that, whereas senior civil servants may serve for a decade or more in a single department, ministers — even cabinet-rank ministers — tend to move departments every couple of years. Although there are clearly some advantages to this ministerial merry-go-round, not least the way in which new blood can reinvigorate tired departments, it can also result in a lack of continuity in policy and a state of constant flux within departments.

The ministerial merry-go-round, 1997–2005

In Dr John Reid, the 2005 cabinet had one of the most itinerant cabinet members of recent years. Reid held six different cabinet posts between 1997 and 2005:

- secretary of state for Scotland
- secretary of state for Northern Ireland
- minister without portfolio (party chair)
- leader of the Commons, Lord President of the Council
- health secretary
- defence secretary

In the 8 years since Labour came to power there have been four different education secretaries (David Blunkett, Estelle Morris, Charles Clarke and Ruth Kelly) and four health secretaries (Frank Dobson, Alan Milburn, John Reid and Patricia Hewitt). With health and education cited as clear priorities for the incoming Labour government in 1997, it is perhaps surprising that no single minister has been present to oversee the significant changes brought to each area of service.

The scale of the ministerial merry-go-round is even more evident with less prestigious posts. On 9 May 2005 the website **egovmonitor.com** noted that the appointment of John Hutton as minister for the Cabinet Office — a cabinet member as Chancellor of the Duchy of Lancaster — made him the fourth minister in 8 months to take leading responsibility for e-government in the UK.

From special adviser to parliamentarian

Although cabinet members must be drawn from parliament, Mr Blair has often fast-tracked those with potential into the Commons as a means of bringing them quickly through the government ranks. In recent years, this process has been particularly overt in the case of former special advisers (see Table 8.1). David Miliband, for example, headed the Policy Unit between 1997 and 2001. His election as an MP in the safe Labour seat of South Shields in 2001 was followed by his appointment as an education minister. In May 2005 he was appointed to the cabinet as minister for communities and local government.

The election of three of Gordon Brown's former special advisers to the Commons in the 2005 general election — Ed Balls, Ed Miliband and Ian Austin — provides another example of an increasingly popular fast track for political advisers whom the prime minister wants to see in government. Former chief economic adviser Ed Balls was described by the *Guardian* as 'the Chancellor in waiting' in a four-page *G2* article on 29 April 2005.

Name	Constituency	Ranking in list of safe Labour seats*
David Miliband	South Shields	38
Ed Miliband	Doncaster North	41
Pat McFadden	Wolverhampton South East	58
Ed Balls	Normanton	121
Kitty Ussher	Burnley	223
Ian Austin	Dudley North	241

* Ranked by % majority in 2005.

Table 8.1 'Spinning' into the Commons

Tony Blair has also elevated key individuals to the Lords as a means of bringing them into government. The industrialist Gus MacDonald was given a peerage and brought into government as minister for business and industry in the Scottish Office in October 1998. Similarly, in 2005, special adviser Andrew Adonis was given a peerage and appointed parliamentary secretary in the Department for Education and Skills. Although Adonis, like Balls and Miliband, was widely regarded as a man of great ability and potential — the *Guardian* described him as 'No. 10's in-house megabrain' (2 August 2005) — the manner of his rise to government inevitably resulted in accusations of spin and cronyism. To an ambitious backbencher, such appointments might also give the impression that the prime minister feels that the talent available in the Commons is limited.

Summary

- Prime ministers rarely have a totally free hand in appointing cabinet members. Certain individuals demand inclusion due to their status or support within the party.

- Prime ministers may face difficulties in exercising their powers of patronage as the end of their premiership draws near. Tony Blair, a case in point, appeared unable to get the cabinet he wanted in May 2005.

- UK ministers are normally generalists rather than specialists. Few ministers stay in one government department for longer than 4 years, although there are some notable recent exceptions to this rule (e.g. Gordon Brown).

- This ministerial merry-go-round has the potential to undermine continuity in the delivery of policy, as well as making it difficult for the ministers in question to establish themselves within a department.

- There has been a marked increase in the number of senior special advisers moving into the legislature (Commons or Lords) and, in some cases, entering government. This may reignite the debate over 'spin' and 'cronyism'.

Chapter 9

A lame-duck premiership?

About this chapter

The Blair premiership has reignited the debate about prime ministerial power and whether the prime minister is too presidential. This chapter addresses key questions about prime ministerial power in 2005:

- Was 2005 a watershed for the Blair premiership?
- Is Blair too presidential?
- What do the first months of his third term tell us about how Blair intends to run this government?
- Should Blair have had such a long holiday in 2005 in the wake of 7 and 21 July?
- Is there a case for reviewing the prime minister's prerogative powers?
- Is the prime minister of 2005 too powerful?

To what extent can May 2005 be seen as a watershed for the Blair premiership?

Tony Blair's time as prime minister could be said to have reached something of a crossroads by May 2005. Domestically, the prime minister's authority appeared to be on the wane:

- Blair's public approval rating was at an all-time low.
- Labour had been returned to power in the general election with the support of only 21.6% of the electorate (a record low) and a greatly reduced Commons majority.
- In the wake of Blair's announcement that he would not be leading his party into a fourth consecutive general election campaign, commentators and some cabinet colleagues appeared to be looking to the succession.

Abroad, the prime minister's close association with the policy in Iraq had affected his credibility:

- The number of UK troops killed in action was fast approaching 100.
- The supposed justification for the war, the readiness of weapons of mass destruction (WMD), had long since been discredited.
- The insurgency in Iraq was gathering pace.

All of this stood in stark contrast to the situation in 1997, when Labour took office on a wave of popular support and Tony Blair appeared unassailable. By

2005, many of those who had previously hailed Blair as presidential were extending the US analogy by characterising him as a 'lame duck' — a premier apparently unable to impose his will on cabinet, party or parliament.

A question of trust?

For many commentators, the 1997 general election hung on the issue of trust. The Conservatives, with their award-winning 'demon eyes' advertisement attacking Blair, portrayed New Labour as a party that could simply not be trusted on the economy or on taxes following the 'Winter of Discontent' of 1979. For Labour, it was the Conservatives who could not be trusted. Allegations of Tory sleaze — particularly in light of the cash-for-questions scandal — had made a mockery of John Major's much heralded 'Back to Basics' campaign. Similarly, Labour's election advertisement targeted the Major government's record on the economy: 'Why trust him on the economy after 22 tax rises?' read the billboard caption next to a picture of a nervous Major biting his nails.

Labour trusted?

'There was no reason left not to trust Labour. All the old "ifs", "buts" and "maybes" had gone.'

Peter Mandelson in the wake of New Labour's victory in 1997.

Although Labour came out on top in 1997, the question of trust is one that persisted throughout Labour's first two terms. Blair's efforts to manage 'the message', not least his reliance on Alastair Campbell and other special advisers, ensured that most of the early headlines showed Blair and the Labour administration in a positive light. This process of personalising and focusing the political debate on the image of the premier does, however, bring with it certain dangers; not least the way in which policy failures come to rest at the door of the prime minister, rather than with the cabinet collectively.

Blair: the 'British president'?

The rise of the 'British presidency'?

'Given the scale, depth and implications of these changes [in the role of the UK premier], it is no exaggeration to declare that the British premiership has to all intents and purposes turned not into a British version of the American presidency, but into an authentically British presidency.'

Source: adapted from M. Foley, 'Presidential politics in Britain', *Talking Politics*, Vol. 6, No. 3, summer 1994.

Features of the 'British presidency'

- A more overt use of the power of patronage as a means of elevating loyalists and marginalising rivals.
- A tendency to limit debate within cabinet.
- An increasing reliance upon cliques, inner cabinets and bilateral meetings.
- A desire to control the media and thereby manage the popular perception of the incumbent prime minister.

Although Tony Blair is hardly the first UK prime minister to be accused of being overly 'presidential', there is clearly something in his manner, style and treatment of colleagues that draws such comments. Michael Foley charted the rise of a new style of prime minister back to the 1970s (see the box above), but it is possible to discern a number of criticisms of Blair's approach that have made talk of a 'British presidency' more pertinent.

What's wrong with Blair?

The following criticisms have been levelled at Blair as prime minister:

- *His concentration of power and influence in the hands of a small group of trusted advisers* — normally unelected special advisers and appointed policy tsars.
- *His diminution of the role of cabinet.* Blair has reduced the frequency and length of cabinet meetings, transformed the cabinet from a decision-making body to a briefing forum, and favoured bilateral meetings — the more informal 'sofa-government' highlighted by the *Guardian* and others.
- *His contempt for parliament.* Blair has a poor attendance record in the Commons. He is willing to use guillotines to limit debate and the Parliament Acts to bully the Lords or, in the case of the ban on hunting with hounds, force through measures that few see as a priority. He has failed to complete Lords reform and has used his powers of patronage to elevate political allies and friends to the interim chamber.
- *His personal conduct.* The late Mo Mowlam characterised Blair's leadership as 'control freakery'. He has been accused of being out of touch with his cabinet, his party and the broader public. The role of his wife, Cherie Booth, has also been strongly criticised (see p. 88).

Time for a new approach?

Although Labour under Blair secured a third consecutive term in office in 2005, the government's reduced Commons majority was widely seen as the electorate's verdict on Blair's leadership — specifically, his stance on Iraq. The prime minister, for his part, appeared to accept their judgement, meeting with

Labour backbenchers shortly after the victory and promising that he would endeavour to listen a good deal more than he had done previously.

Despite such assurances, however, Blair was soon antagonising backbenchers again by appointing No.10 aide Andrew Adonis first to the Lords and then straight into a post as junior education minister. Adonis is a former SDP activist who had been closely associated with policies such as the introduction of city academies and top-up fees during his time as a special adviser. His appointment was, according to George Jones of the *Daily Telegraph*, a clear indication that the prime minister intended to keep just as close a rein on policy as he had previously. The *Guardian* went so far as to suggest that Adonis might come to be regarded the 'real' secretary of state for education, rather than the official incumbent, Ruth Kelly.

Having announced prior to the May election that he would not be leading the Labour Party into a fourth general election, Blair had to fight against the creeping sense that he was a lame-duck prime minister. Blair's biographer, Anthony Seldon, felt that the prime minister was clearly gearing up to secure a lasting legacy in August 2005. In an article entitled 'Revitalised Blair plans to get radical' (*The Times*, 28 August), Seldon and Robert Winnett felt that changes were likely to come quickly in key areas of policy. These are given in the box below.

Securing Blair's legacy

Healthcare
- Increased use of the private sector to provide services for patients.
- Rapid expansion in the number of foundation hospitals.

Education
- Rapid expansion of city academies.
- New national standards for such academies.
- Steady removal of schools from local authority control.

Law and order
- New performance targets and even league tables for the police.
- More prison sentences for those found guilty of antisocial behaviour.

Source: adapted from *The Times*, 28 August 2005.

Such moves would be certain to prompt backbench and possibly cabinet rebellion, yet Blair's impending departure may have the effect of making his potential successors, chief among them Gordon Brown, more loyal in the coming months as they endeavour to make themselves 'look the part'. In any event, Blair's impending departure means that he simply does not have the time to take things slowly.

Blair's exit strategy

'Government sources say that Blair is worried that New Labour has not yet changed the country significantly to guarantee his personal legacy...He fears that if he hands over too early, it could be the chancellor who is credited in the history books with radically reforming the health service, education, pensions and transport.'

Source: Toby Helms and Rachel Sylvester, 'Blair plans exit strategy to ensure reform', *Daily Telegraph*, 23 April 2005.

A promising start? The first months of New Labour's third term

The first 2 months of Labour's historic third term saw the prime minister taking a definite lead. Although his cabinet reshuffle had not gone entirely to plan, he continued to impress on the international stage:

- He offered the EU leadership and direction when the ratification of the new constitution stalled.
- He used the UK's presidency of the G8 to address the issue of debt relief in the developing world.
- He flew out to Singapore on the eve of the G8 summit to 'press the flesh' and thereby secure the 2012 Olympics for London.

According to the Bagehot column in *The Economist* (16 July 2005), even Conservative MPs found it hard to contain their admiration for the prime minister's handling of these three set-piece interventions. In the event, however, the announcement that London had won the Olympic bid represented something of a high-water mark for the prime minister, with things going somewhat awry thereafter.

Bombs, Barbados and Booth: a problematic summer for the prime minister

The terrorist attacks in London on 7 and 21 July 2005 reopened the debate on the efficacy of the war in Iraq. Prior to the Anglo-American action in the Gulf, it had been the prime minister's contention that:

- Iraq had WMD that were ready for immediate use.
- Military action in Iraq would lessen, rather than heighten, the risk of terrorist attack on the UK mainland.

With the WMD claims long since discredited, the attacks on 7 July struck at the heart of the second assertion. Official advice which was leaked later appeared to suggest that action in Iraq might make terrorist attacks in the UK *more* likely; it was followed by the release of a pre-recorded video by one of the 7 July attackers, making an explicit link between UK action in Iraq and the London attack. Both dealt damaging blows to the prime minister's credibility and gave a fillip to those inside and outside parliament who had opposed military action from the outset.

Although the secrecy surrounding the location of the prime minister's extended summer break in 2005 was, of course, mere trivia when compared to the attacks in London, it added to the sense that the prime minister remained somehow out of touch with the public mood. Blair's annual summer holidays have long caused controversy and, as Alice Miles pointed out in *The Times* on 17 August, it seemed somewhat perverse that he should be enjoying such a long break in a 'secret' location at the same time that Londoners were facing the fear of sudden death every time they boarded the Tube. 'After all,' she argued, 'al-Qaeda knows that I am on the underground every morning, and that so are you, or your brother, your wife, your son. They, we, are all open targets. I think the prime minister should accept the increased risk of this summer alongside us.'

The prime minister's extended absence also meant he was away at the time of former colleague Robin Cook's death and subsequent funeral. Although few would have taken it upon themselves to use the funeral to speak out against the prime minister's absence in the manner that Channel 4's racing pundit John McCririck did, the note he struck found resonance in the popular press, just as Gordon Brown's eulogy appeared to enhance his own status as prime minister in waiting. By 8 September 2005, TUC leader Brendan Barber was arguing that Blair should step down in favour of Brown sooner rather than later.

The prime minister's wife, Cherie Booth, continued to provide the mass media with the means by which to attack both her and her husband. The publication of her book, *The Goldfish Bowl: Married to the Prime Minister 1955–1997*, though not drawing on her own experiences directly, was widely panned as an ill-judged attempt to cash in on her husband's position while he was still in office. Her lectures championing civil liberties and highlighting the dangers of governments over-reacting to the threat of terrorism were also widely reported. Although most of the editorial comment was favourable, the concerns she raised again appeared to question the government's approach in dealing with suspected terrorists.

Problems with the No. 10 team?

Labour's historic third election victory in 2005 brought with it a further changing of the guard at Downing Street. On 2 August 2005, the *Guardian* reported that there was a 'Testing month [ahead] for the new team at No. 10', as Tony Blair jetted off for his extended summer break. Although key figures remained in place, other long-term aides departed their posts. The only comfort, perhaps, was that two of those leaving, Pat McFadden and Andrew Adonis, were entering parliament (as MP and peer, respectively) and were likely, therefore, to retain an input.

Should I stay or should I go? Key aides at No. 10 in May 2005

Staying	Going
Jonathan Powell, chief of staff	Sally Morgan, director of political and government relations
David Hill, communications director	
Tom Kelly, No. 10 spokesman	Pat McFadden, political secretary
	Andrew Adonis, No. 10 adviser

Sally Morgan's departure was the one that many saw as the most significant. Although she had moved from her post as political secretary to become director of political and government relations in 2001, she had remained a central figure. Her departure in 2005 saw her various responsibilities divided among three individuals — Matthew Taylor (on policy), Jo Gibbons (organising events) and Ruth Turner (government relations).

Sally Morgan

'Sally has been there for so long and was so important that her departure left a very big hole to fill…Forget the job title, she was Tony's political adviser, counsellor to the cabinet, a person whose shoulder they could cry on. They all knew they were speaking to someone who had Tony's ear.'

A 'Downing Street veteran' quoted in the *Guardian*, 2 August 2005.

Prerogative powers in question?

Sensing the prime minister's vulnerability, perhaps, both opposition parties and the House of Lords questioned the prime minister's use of prerogative powers in 2005. Although the prime minister's diminution of cabinet in recent years represents one aspect of the much heralded rise of the 'British presidency', his use of prerogative powers has also been evident in two other areas:

- Patronage — most visibly with appointments to the civil service and to the Lords.
- Foreign affairs — most controversially with regard to the so-called 'war power' (see the box on p. 90).

Prime ministerial appointments to the Lords under the prerogative powers of the monarch increased significantly following the first stage of Lords reform, but it is the elevation of individuals like Andrew Adonis that has drawn particular criticism. In the case of Adonis, this sense was heightened by the speed with which he was installed as a junior minister for education.

In the area of civil service appointments, too, Blair caused controversy by presiding over an unprecedented expansion in the number of politically appointed special advisers. Some within the Labour Party defended the proliferation of special advisers as a means of controlling or, failing that, bypassing a civil service that had become politicised during 18 years of Conservative

government. It is ironic, therefore, that Labour's use of special advisers itself led the Liberal Democrats and others to accuse the party of politicising the civil service to the point at which a new Civil Service Act was made necessary (see the box below).

'The Real Alternative': the Liberal Democrats and prime ministerial power

'A Liberal Democrat government will:

- cut back the prime minister's powers of patronage…with a predominantly elected second chamber
- bring in a War Powers Act to require parliament's authority before a government takes Britain to war, thus making prime ministers accountable in their use of prerogative powers
- introduce a Civil Service Act that will present a barrier to politicisation of the civil service'

Source: adapted from the Liberal Democrat manifesto, 2005.

It is Prime Minister Blair's activities in the field of foreign affairs, however, that have most often seen him described as presidential. Although Labour's foreign secretaries between 1997 and 2005 were both well-regarded and experienced political heavyweights (Robin Cook and Jack Straw), Blair — perhaps more than any incumbent since Churchill — has appeared keen to make his own mark on the international stage.

The foreign policy prime minister

US presidents facing difficulties in domestic affairs often seek solace in diplomacy. The same could be said of Tony Blair's premiership. The prime minister's globe-trotting style, his willingness to encroach upon the foreign secretary's brief, and his obvious desire to be statesmanlike all contrast sharply with a domestic programme that has stagnated somewhat.

The war power

- In law, the prime minister is not required to seek Commons approval either to take the country to war or to commit the UK to international treaties.
- Although John Major presented the Maastricht Treaty to the Commons as a virtual vote of confidence, his legal team advised him that the treaty could be made law with or without Commons approval.
- Similarly, although the Commons vote on war in Iraq went Blair's way, the constitutional power to declare war is not with the legislature, as it is in the USA, but with the executive.
- It is this reality that led the Liberal Democrats to call for the introduction of a formal War Powers Act in their 2005 general election manifesto.

The prime minister's regular foreign visits have kept him in the media spotlight, most notably over Iraq, where his high profile contrasted sharply with Jack Straw's relative anonymity. Blair's 'staunch and steadfast' support of the US position on Iraq was rewarded with the Congressional Gold Medal in July 2003, making him the first Briton to win the honour since Winston Churchill, who was awarded posthumously in 1969. As J. J. Scarisbrick noted in his landmark biography of Henry VIII, however, 'a reputation is not easy to make with a foreign policy', as one can so rarely control enough of the variables to ensure success.

As Iraq unravelled, Blair's personal association with the policy made the closeness of his relationship with George W. Bush a political embarrassment rather than an asset. *The Times* suggested that this could be one reason why Blair had yet to collect his medal as of 27 August 2005.

Despite setbacks over the much heralded 'war on terror', Tony Blair has also been active over the issues of climate change and aid for Africa. The prime minister was the driving force behind the formation of the Commission for Africa, and used the UK's presidency of the G8 in 2005 to focus attention on the problems facing the continent. Blair has also pursued beneficial trade links with foreign powers. In a visit to New Delhi on 8 September 2005, for example, the prime minister announced a £10 million scholarship fund to support student exchanges between India and the UK.

How powerful was the UK prime minister in 2005?

Notwithstanding Tony Blair's obvious ease on the diplomatic stage, there were good reasons for concluding that the prime minister had indeed become something of a lame duck by the summer of 2005. Blair's public announcement of his decision not to lead his party into the next general election inevitably led commentators to focus on the question of the succession, as illustrated amply by the media postmortem that followed his decision not to return from holiday to attend Robin Cook's funeral. By his own admission, the prime minister now has a 'limited shelf-life'; the question is clearly one of 'when?' rather than 'if?'

As the media obsession with the prime minister has diminished, the role of the cabinet appears to have become central once more. On the *Today* programme on 18 September, for example, it was reported that 'the cabinet' would be considering whether or not to go ahead with the proposed revaluation of properties for the purposes of council tax. Although it would be premature on the basis of this evidence alone to conclude that the 'British presidency' is dead and 'cabinet government' is reborn, there has clearly been a change of emphasis in the media and, perhaps, in government itself.

Summary

- The view that the prime minister is merely *primus inter pares*, already open to question in Bagehot's time, is now something of an anachronism.

- Recent prime ministers have used their prerogative powers, and the spotlight afforded them by the rise of the mass media, to adopt a style and approach that is quasi-presidential.

- Despite this, the prime minister's position at the apex of the UK political system makes the incumbent particularly vulnerable to the unexpected. As Harold Macmillan acknowledged, 'events, dear boy, events' are the biggest problem facing any government. Although the media spotlight can help a dynamic and charismatic prime minister consolidate his or her position, the media are equally adept at bringing leaders down.

- As with the US president, prime ministers who see their domestic policy agendas thwarted often look to secure a lasting legacy for themselves in the field of foreign affairs.

- The prime minister's use of prerogative powers is coming under increased scrutiny.

- The inevitable sense that Tony Blair is something of a lame-duck premier has offered the possibility of an enhanced role for cabinet.

Parliament: legislature or 'rubber stamp'?

About this chapter

New Labour's efforts to reform parliament, particularly the Lords, since 1997 have been criticised either for going too far or for not going far enough. This chapter addresses parliamentary reform in the context of the 2005 general election.

- What did the parties say about parliamentary reform in their election manifestos?
- How might the composition of the Lords and the Commons change in the future?
- What are the prospects for changes in powers or effectiveness?
- How effective is the Modernisation Committee?
- Will parliament change in the near future?

Prospects for parliamentary reform in 2005

Although Labour all but fulfilled its 1997 promise to remove hereditary peers from the Lords, leaving just 92 hereditaries in a transitional chamber, the party's efforts to reform the upper house ran aground thereafter. Similarly, the changes made to Commons organisation and procedure have been widely criticised as being concerned more with the day-to-day practicalities of organising the House's business than with bringing the UK's lower chamber into the twenty-first century.

The 2005 general election gave all three main UK parties the opportunity to try and set the course of future parliamentary reform. What did they offer?

Labour manifesto pledges
- Remove remaining hereditary peers.
- Hold a free vote on the composition of the reformed chamber.
- Codify key Lords conventions and legislate to limit to 60 days the time that most bills spend in the Lords.
- Improve the effectiveness of Commons scrutiny.

Conservative manifesto pledges
- Seek cross-party consensus for a 'substantially elected' Lords.
- Commons to have 20% fewer MPs; Scottish MPs to be barred from voting on English laws. Ideally, 'English votes for English laws'.
- Enhance select committees and make time for the proper scrutiny of bills.

Liberal Democrat manifesto pledges

● A predominantly elected upper chamber to replace the Lords.
● Strengthen parliament's powers of scrutiny over the executive, including enhanced select committees in the Commons.

What is wrong with parliament?

The proposals outlined in the manifestos reflected concerns regarding the shape and effectiveness of parliament, which all three parties held in common in 2005:

● There was a consensus that the Labour programme of Lords reform that began with the removal of all but 92 of the 700 or so hereditary peers must be completed. However, the parties differed on the precise composition of the new chamber.
● There was broad agreement that the whole issue of scrutiny of the executive needs to be addressed, with a strengthening of the system of select committees the most likely solution.

Although the problems facing parliament are probably more fundamental than these two areas alone, being rooted in the UK's fusion of legislature and

Executive dominance unpicked

■ Governments commanding large Commons majorities are able to circumvent parliamentary procedure.

■ The work of the majority party's whips and the imposition of guillotines on parliamentary debate allow governments to force through bills.

■ The Lords' power to block government initiatives is limited by the Parliament Acts and by the Salisbury Doctrine. The Lords is, at best, a revising chamber.

■ The powers of scrutiny held by UK standing committees and departmental select committees are weak in comparison to those exercised by US standing committees.

Lord Hailsham on 'elective dictatorship'

'There has been a continuous enlargement of the scale and range of government itself [accompanied by] a change in the relative influence of the different elements in government, so as to place all the effective powers in the hands of one of them [i.e. the prime minister]. In other words, the checks and balances, which in practice used to prevent abuse, have now disappeared. [These] changes have operated in [one] direction — to increase the extent to which elective dictatorship is a fact, and not just a lawyer's theory. The government controls parliament, and not parliament the government. Until recently, debate and argument dominated the parliamentary scene. Now, it is the whips and the party caucus. More and more, debate, where it is not actually curtailed, is becoming a ritual dance, sometimes interspersed with catcalls.'

Source: adapted from The Richard Dimbleby Lecture, *Listener*, 21 October 1976.

executive (as indicated in the box above), our purpose here is to consider likely developments in the year ahead, rather than revisit the path well trodden in standard textbooks.

How might the composition of parliament change in the next few years?

The House of Lords

The government is already coming under pressure over the tortuously slow pace of Lords reform (see the box below). It seems likely, therefore, that the next year will see Labour making efforts to fulfil its 2005 manifesto pledge by attempting to:

* Remove the remaining 92 hereditary peers.
* Allow a free vote on the future composition of the second chamber.

Government urged to get moving on Lords reform

'Campaigners today called on the government to press ahead with reform of the House of Lords, on the 94th birthday of the Parliament Act. Elect the Lords, a coalition of organisations committed to democratic reform of the upper house...pointed out that...when [the Parliament Act] was first introduced it was only intended as an interim measure prior to the House of Lords being replaced by a second chamber "composed on a popular basis".

Peter Facey, Elect the Lords' national co-ordinator, said, "Labour has repeatedly promised to complete reform of the House of Lords and the other two parties support a substantially elected second chamber. After 8 years of debate and muddle, there can be no more time for delay."'

Source: adapted from the *Guardian*, 10 August 2005.

The government will, however, face serious problems in both areas. First, as the Lords is unlikely to approve the removal of the residual hereditaries without a fight, the government may well be forced to consider using the Parliament Act. It is by no means certain, however, that the courts would uphold the use of the Parliament Act in forcing through such a significant

---

Limits on the Parliament Act

'Senior ministers are bracing themselves for a fresh showdown if the Law Lords endorse a [February] ruling [from the Court of Appeal] challenging the government's right to overrule the upper house. Though the court upheld the legality of the use of the 1949 Parliament Act to force through a ban on hunting, the court concluded that "the greater the scale of the constitutional change proposed, the more likely that it would fall outside the powers contained in the 1911 Act". This could leave a question mark over the government's ability to use the Parliament Act to remove the remaining 92 hereditary peers.'

Source: adapted from the *Guardian*, 3 August 2005.

---

constitutional change. With the 1949 Parliament Act having itself been forced through using the 1911 Act, a question mark hangs over the former's legality. Though the Court of Appeal upheld the use of the 1949 Act in forcing through the ban on hunting with hounds, it delivered a clear warning regarding the future use of the Act.

Second, there is a real possibility that a free vote on the future composition of the Lords will go the same way as the last votes on the issue in 2003, when all of the proposed models were rejected. This would leave Lords reform exactly where it is now — in limbo.

The House of Commons

Although it is unlikely that the Conservatives' call for 20% fewer MPs will be realised in the next few years, the composition of the Commons may well change in other respects. Recent elections have, for example, seen a marked increase in the number of women MPs in parliament. Whereas in 1987 there were only 41 female MPs, in 2005, 128 were returned in an election where 20.3% of all candidates were female. Although only five black MPs were returned in 2005, it is significant that 6% of all candidates were, according to Operation Black Vote, from ethnic minorities. This is broadly in line with the 7.9% of the population who were from ethnic minorities at the time of the 2001 census.

It is likely that the average age of MPs, 52.3 years in April 2005, will fall considerably over the next two parliamentary terms. Although the youngest MP elected in May 2005, Liberal Democrat Jo Swinson (aged 25), was one of only a handful of 'twenty-somethings' returned in the general election, the major parties already appear to be looking to younger candidates in an attempt to appeal to younger voters, many of whom have not turned out in recent elections. On 25 July 2005, the *Guardian* ran with the headline 'Labour asks senior MPs to make way for the young' (see the box below). Perhaps the candidature and election of former Labour special advisers such as Ed Balls (aged 38) should therefore be seen as evidence of this trend towards promoting the young, rather than as evidence of cronyism.

A new breed of MPs?

'Senior Labour officials are hoping to…ease out senior MPs and allow younger activists to begin campaigning as part of a general overhaul of the party undertaken in light of its vastly reduced majority. The party also hopes to use its reorganisation to promote women and people from black or [other] ethnic minorities. The party has set itself a challenging target of ensuring that 40% of its MPs are women after the next election. At present, women only form 28% of the parliamentary party.'

Source: adapted from the *Guardian*, 25 July 2005.

How might the powers and effectiveness of the legislature be enhanced in the next few years?

A new role for a new upper chamber?

Even without further reform, the Lords had already begun to assert itself by the summer of 2005. Senior peers were, for example, said to be considering whether or not they should hold to the Salisbury Doctrine (see the box below). In early September, Charter 88 voiced support for the House of Lords Constitution Committee's stated intention to examine the use of the royal prerogative, with respect to the government's ability to go to war without parliament's approval.

A move towards a fully or largely elected second chamber would have serious knock-on effects for the legitimacy and, perhaps, the powers of the chamber. A largely elected chamber might well claim its own mandate and be even less willing to defer to government and the Commons. This reality is, perhaps, behind Tony Blair's preference for a wholly appointed chamber and Labour's 2005 manifesto commitment to codify Lords conventions and limit the time available for the Lords' consideration of bills.

Some limitations on the Lords

The Parliament Acts, 1911 and 1949

The 1911 Parliament Act replaced the Lords' right to veto legislation with the power to delay bills for 2 years. At the same time, the Lords were effectively prevented from vetoing, amending or delaying money bills. The Parliament Act of 1949 reduced the power of delay to one parliamentary session.

The Salisbury Doctrine

Dating from 1945, the Salisbury Doctrine put in place the principle that the Lords — as an unelected chamber — should not oppose government bills at second reading where the government has established a clear electoral mandate to act by including a measure in its manifesto.

Better Commons scrutiny over the executive

The departmental select committees introduced in 1979, although widely admired, have struggled to hold the executive to account in the manner effected by their US counterparts. Their relative impotence is the result of a number of interlocking factors. For example:

- Committee membership has been manipulated by the party whips, even to the point where efforts have been made to replace awkward chairs with party loyalists. Thus the government attempted to prevent Gwyneth Dunwoody (Transport Select Committee) and Donald Anderson (Foreign Affairs Select Committee) retaining their roles as chairs in 2001.
- Committees do not have the power to force ministers to give evidence before them; for instance, Tony Blair refused to give evidence to the Public Administration Select Committee on the Ministerial Code in 2001.

A number of schemes to enhance the scope and powers of UK select committees have been floated in recent years:

- In 2000 the Commons' Liaison Committee, which comprises chairs of the 34 departmental select committees, produced a report entitled *Shifting the Balance*. The report suggested taking control of the nomination of select committee members away from the party whips. The government rejected this and most of the committee's other proposals, although some re-emerged in modified form in 2002 as the House Modernisation Committee's proposals (see the box below).

- *The Norton Report* (2000), which came from the Commission to Strengthen Parliament, set up under Lord Norton by the then Conservative leader William Hague, recommended the strengthening and broadening of the system of select committees. This, it was argued, would allow for greater scrutiny of legislation and might also help to improve financial efficiency. It would make the work of government and parliament more transparent, allowing for greater public appreciation of parliament's work. Specifically, the report supported the view that committee appointments should be taken out of the hands of the whips.

- *The Newton Report* (2001) was the product of a commission set up by the Hansard Society under Lord Newton. The report concluded that greater accountability would necessitate the strengthening of the select committee system, as well as a greater willingness to communicate to the broader public in a sincere and comprehensible manner.

Although all three main parties proposed enhancing the work of select committees in their 2005 general election manifestos, specific details were less evident.

What are the options?

In February 2002, the Modernisation Committee made a number of proposals regarding the ways in which the work of select committees might be enhanced.

Recommendations of the Modernisation Committee

Committee appointments: the establishment of a Committee of Selection under the Chair of Ways and Means, with the majority of its members being drawn from the chair's panel and its membership set by standing order.
Motion rejected 209:195

Increased resources: the establishment of a specialist unit of staff to assist committees with consideration of departmental expenditure and pre-legislative scrutiny, and increased staff for select committees.
No vote

Core tasks: a list of principal objectives for select committees with annual reports reporting performance against these tasks.
Motion passed

An alternative career structure: an additional salary to be paid to the chairs of select committees and a term limit on holding the chair.
Motion passed

An increased role for backbenchers: select committees to be increased in size to 15 members, thus giving more MPs select committee posts.
No vote

Connecting with the public: select committees to be renamed as 'scrutiny committees' and their reports redesigned to make them attractive to readers.
No vote

Source: adapted from Lucinda Maer, 'Modernisation of the House of Commons 1997–2005' (House of Commons Research Paper 05/46) 14 June 2005.

If such committees are to scrutinise the executive effectively, however, two requirements are clear:

- They must be free from the control of the party whips.
- They must have the power to demand that ministers and others come before them (i.e. the legal power of subpoena).

If nothing else, the first requirement should be self-evident from the way in which the whips were said to have interfered in the supposedly free vote on the Modernisation Committee's first and probably most important recommendation, that on committee appointments, resulting in its defeat.

A missed opportunity? The Commons Modernisation Committee

'The Select Committee on Modernisation of the House of Commons was established in June 1997 and has been chaired by the leader of the House of Commons. It is said that having a cabinet minister on the committee has proven to be a "double-edged sword". Although the [committee's] recommendations have a good chance of being agreed to by the House, the nature of the committee's recommendations could be seen as reflecting the will of the government to pass its business through the House efficiently rather than aiming to strengthen parliament's scrutiny role.

In a June 2005 paper for the Hansard Society entitled 'New Politics, New Parliament? A review of the modernisation of parliamentary procedures and practices since 1997', Alex Brazier, Matthew Flinders and Declan McHugh concluded that "a glance at the Modernisation Committee's work over the last 8 years...illustrates that, at least for the duration of the 1997 parliament, its focus was generally on legislation and procedural issues...timetabling and the upgrading of media facilities, rather than the more fundamental matter of shifting power back to the legislature".'

Source: adapted from Lucinda Maer, 'Modernisation of the House of Commons 1997–2005' (House of Commons Research Paper 05/46), 14 June 2005.

What other changes are likely in the short to mid term?

The most obvious and immediate change to the scope of parliament's powers will be the removal of the Lords' judicial function with the creation of a new UK Supreme Court. The creation of this court, together with the long-planned abolition of the role of Lord Chancellor and the creation of an Independent Judicial Appointments Commission, will provide a more formal separation between legislature, executive and judiciary.

Although the new court will not be afforded the same status as its US counterpart, there being no supreme and codified constitution for it to hold over parliamentary statute, it will mark a significant watershed in the evolution of the UK constitution.

Committee appointments and accountability

'You don't hold the government to account by giving top committee jobs to yes-men.'

Richard Benyon, MP for Newbury and member of the Home Affairs Select Committee, in a talk to students at Portcullis House, Westminster, 27 September 2005.

Conclusion

Although this update reflects the somewhat pessimistic view of the state of parliament promulgated in the major parties' 2005 general election manifestos, there are in fact significant grounds for optimism regarding the future of the UK legislature.

The removal of over 600 hereditary peers from the Lords in 1998, for example, does not appear to have seen the upper house transformed into a chamber of placemen and lick-spittles. In the 2003–04 parliamentary session (November to November), the Lords tabled 9,602 amendments to bills, passing 3,344 and defeating the government in 61 votes.

Similarly, the Lords' willingness to review the Salisbury Doctrine, their questioning of the prime minister's use of the royal prerogative, and their treatment of the revised anti-terrorist legislation hardly lend support to the notion that the chamber has ceased to serve a purpose.

The Commons has also become more robust in its treatment of government bills, despite Labour's considerable Commons majority up to May 2005. The scale of the rebellions over the war in Iraq, foundation hospitals, top-up fees and city academies — though all ultimately doomed — will have given the government considerable food for thought. With Labour's majority down to 65 following the 2005 general election, it is possible that we will see a more assertive chamber in the coming months.

Summary

- Despite early attempts to remove hereditary peers, parliamentary reform over Labour's first two terms in office has not lived up to expectations.

- The problem of Lords reform remains an intractable one.

- Effective Commons scrutiny of the executive is hindered by the UK's fusion of executive and legislature, and by the power of party, as exercised by the whips.

- It is likely to prove extremely hard to make meaningful enhancements to the role of select committees.

- Despite this, the UK parliament is still capable of holding the government to account. Indeed, there is some evidence to suggest that the UK legislature is less of a 'rubber stamp' than it was 8 years ago.

Constitutional reform: a stalled revolution?

About this chapter

In 1997 Labour came to power on the back of a manifesto that had promised a wide-ranging programme of constitutional reform. By 2005, many felt that this programme had stalled.

This chapter looks at six broad areas of constitutional reform. For each area it addresses three key questions:

- What reforms, if any, did the three main parties offer in their 2005 general election manifestos?
- What prompted them to make such proposals?
- How likely is it that any of these proposals will be implemented in the short to medium term?

The issue of constitutional change in 2005

At the time of the 2005 general election, many commentators took the opportunity to assess New Labour's achievements during its first 8 years in office. Much of their commentary centred, not surprisingly, on the administration's record in the field of constitutional reform.

What is a constitution?

A constitution is a body of rules that defines the manner in which a state or society is organised. It sets out the way in which sovereign power is distributed between the government and the people, and between the government's constituent parts. A constitution provides a framework upon which more complex rules, structures and processes can be built.

Constitutional reform thus consists of measures that seek to change the relationships:

- between people and state
- between different state institutions
- between central and sub-national government
- between central and supranational government

Labour's 1997 manifesto had set out a wide-ranging programme of constitutional change (see the box below). Some analysts had even drawn comparisons between this and proposals made by civil liberties groups such as Charter 88 a decade earlier.

Labour's promises in 1997

Labour claimed 'We will clean up politics' by promising the following:

- An end to the hereditary principle in the House of Lords.
- Reform of party funding to end sleaze.
- Devolved power in Scotland and Wales.
- Elected mayors for London and other cities.
- More independent but accountable local government.
- Freedom of information and guaranteed human rights.

Source: adapted from the 1997 Labour Party manifesto.

Although Labour had delivered on most of the firm commitments it made in its 1997 manifesto by the time of the 2005 general election, many felt that the remodelling of the UK's constitution lacked coherence and that far too many projects remained incomplete. As a consequence, all three major parties proposed significant constitutional changes in their 2005 election manifestos. Labour focused on reviewing the efficacy of the changes made during its first 8 years in office and completing unfinished projects, rather than initiating major new changes; the main opposition parties argued that further changes were necessary.

The 2005 manifesto proposals made by the three main UK parties related to six broad questions:

(1) How might the executive be reformed?

(2) How might the programme of parliamentary reform be taken forward?

(3) How should the UK's relationship with the EU develop?

(4) How should the devolution project be taken forward?

(5) How should power be divided between central, regional and local government?

(6) How should the programme of electoral reform introduced since 1997 progress?

The executive

What prompted the 2005 manifesto promises?

With Labour in power, it was always likely that the main proposals for reform in this area would come from the opposition parties. The Conservatives' promise of limits on government-imposed regulation were hardly ground breaking, reflecting as it did their desire to champion 'small government' in the

face of Labour's supposed 'big government' interventionism. The party's suggestion that the UK should follow the lead of the USA in establishing a new ministry of homeland security provoked a degree of media interest, but it was widely seen as an attempt to bring the traditional Tory issue of security to the fore, rather than as a proposal that would significantly reduce the threat posed by terrorists.

Conservative	Labour	Liberal Democrats
■ Creation of a new 'homeland security minister'. ■ Controls on the extent and costs of government-imposed regulation.		■ A War Powers Act and Civil Service Act to limit the prime minister's prerogative powers. ■ Abolish the Department of Trade and Industry and cut the number of ministers by one third.

Source: adapted from *Monitor*, the bulletin of University College London's Constitution Unit (www.ucl.ac.uk/constitution-unit), April 2005.

Table 11.1 Manifesto promises 2005

The Liberal Democrats focused more squarely on the way in which the prime minister has come to exercise the monarch's prerogative powers, both in the domestic sphere and abroad. At home, the prime minister's use of politically appointed special advisers — which some saw as part of a wider process of politicisation in the civil service — prompted the Liberal Democrats to call for a new Civil Service Act. Similarly, they argued, the prime minister should no longer be permitted to wage war and enter the UK into treaties without parliamentary ratification. The Liberal Democrats thus proposed a formal US-style War Powers Act as a means of subjecting the prime minister to greater scrutiny in this area.

Will these proposals be implemented in the short to medium term?

Labour's victory in the 2005 general election has made significant change in this area unlikely, in the short term at least. It is interesting to note, however, that the House of Lords has now taken up the baton regarding prime ministerial power, stating its intention to examine the use of prerogative powers — particularly with respect to UK action in Iraq.

The legislature

What prompted the 2005 manifesto promises?

The 2005 manifestos saw both opposition parties looking to strengthen the powers of parliament and thereby enhance scrutiny of the executive. Proposals to enhance the scope and power of departmental select committees, though hardly novel, were well received in the media. The opposition parties' enthusiasm for a largely elected second chamber also reflected a desire to provide a check to Labour's legislative ambitions.

Conservative Party	Labour Party	Liberal Democrats
■ Work towards a 'substantially elected' Lords. ■ Commons to have 20% fewer MPs and Scottish MPs to be barred from voting on English laws. ■ Enhanced select committees.	■ Abolish remaining hereditary peers and hold a free vote on composition of reformed chamber. ■ Examine Lords' powers of scrutiny. ■ Improve effectiveness of Commons' scrutiny.	■ A predominantly elected upper chamber to replace the Lords. ■ Enhanced select committees to enhance Commons' scrutiny.

Source: adapted from *Monitor*, the bulletin of University College London's Constitution Unit (**www.ucl.ac.uk/constitution-unit**), April 2005.

Table 11.2 Manifesto promises 2005

According to the Constitution Unit's *Monitor*, Labour was, in contrast, looking to 'codify Lords procedural conventions and limit [the] time most bills spend in [the] Lords'. Such moves were widely seen as an attempt to limit the Lords' scrutiny of the executive.

Although Labour offered a free vote on the future composition of the second chamber, it appeared to offer no suggestion as to what would happen if, as was the case in 2003, all of the options for a remodelled chamber were rejected.

Will these proposals be implemented in the short to medium term?
Although enhancements to Commons departmental select committees have been a recurring theme in party manifestos over recent years, the details of precisely what this might entail have often been far harder to establish. The last attempt to make significant changes to the composition and procedure of select committees, the Commons Modernisation Committee's recommendations of 2002, were hamstrung by the whips' willingness to work behind the scenes and block a measure that would have removed the whips' own role in shaping the composition of such committees.

A question mark also hangs over proposals for completing the remodelling of the upper chamber. Although the House of Lords Act (1999) went some way towards meeting Labour's 1997 manifesto pledge, its 2001 manifesto commitment to create a 'more representative and democratic' second chamber appears no closer to realisation now than it did then. The limited nature of Labour's 2005 manifesto commitment tends to support the view that the party has neither the will nor a way to resolve the impasse over Lords' reform.

Labour and Lords reform, 1997–2005
■ Labour's 1997 manifesto commitment to remove the rights of hereditary peers to sit and vote in the House of Lords was not tied to further Lords reform.

■ The House of Lords Act (1999) removed the right of over 600 hereditary peers to sit and vote in the Lords.

- The Weatherill Amendment allowed 92 hereditaries to stay on in a transitional House prior to the completion of Lords reform.

- Critics argued that the move from a part-appointed and part-hereditary chamber to one that was wholly appointed simply provided Tony Blair with the opportunity to fill the chamber with his supporters.

- In 2003 all eight proposals for a new chamber, ranging from outright abolition to a wholly elected chamber, were rejected.

- Despite Labour largely fulfilling its 1997 commitments on Lords reform, the remodelling of the second chamber remained unfinished in October 2005.

The European Union

What prompted the 2005 manifesto promises?

All three main UK parties entered the 2005 campaign with the promise that the UK's ratification of the new EU constitution would be dependent upon a nationwide referendum. For Labour this commitment represented something of an about-turn from the position it had held a year earlier. Initially, the government had maintained that the new constitution was simply a 'tidying-up exercise'. Consequently, it argued, the adoption of the new constitution should be no more be dependent upon a public vote than was the Maastricht Treaty some 14 years earlier.

Conservatives	Liberal Democrats	Labour
- 'No' to the euro. - A referendum on the EU constitution, but Conservatives will oppose it. - Renegotiate the opt-out from the Social Chapter and take back control over asylum policy from Brussels.	- Keen on the EU constitution and the euro, but referendums before either.	- Referendums before joining the euro or accepting the EU constitution.

Source: adapted from *Monitor*, the bulletin of University College London's Constitution Unit (www.ucl.ac.uk/constitution-unit), April 2005.

Table 11.3 Manifesto promises 2005

By the time of the 2005 general election, however, Tony Blair had apparently been convinced that a referendum would indeed be necessary. This concession was widely seen as a political necessity, rather than being founded in law or merit. Labour, it was argued, could not afford to allow the constitution to become a key issue in the campaign, particularly as the two main opposition parties were already committed to a public vote on the matter. With all three parties entering the election with the promise of a referendum, the potential for the issue to become a major vote-loser for Labour was greatly reduced — just as the offer of a referendum over possible UK adoption of the single currency had diffused the issue ahead of the 1997 general election.

Will these proposals be implemented in the short to medium term?
Although the three main parties took different stances on future UK relations with Europe, the main bone of contention — the ratification of the new EU constitution — was removed by the French rejection of the treaty establishing the new constitution in a referendum on 29 May 2005 and the Dutch rejection that followed 3 days later. By October 2005, even long-time Europhile and serial Conservative leadership contender Kenneth Clarke was acknowledging that the constitution was dead and accepting that the UK would not be adopting the euro for at least 10 years. In October 2005, all three parties remained committed to holding referendums before UK ratification of any new EU constitution or UK entry into the single currency.

The fuss over asylum, fuelled by the fear of mass immigration following the accession of ten new EU states in 2005, and the supposed link between asylum and terrorism, also appeared to have subsided somewhat by the end of 2005. Some suggested that the Conservatives' decision to focus their 2005 general election campaign on such issues said more about the influence of Australian political consultant Lynton Crosby, and party polling of floating voters in key marginals, than it did about the underlying public mood.

Devolution

What prompted the 2005 manifesto promises?
In 2005 the three main parties' positions on the future of devolved bodies were shaped by their very different perspectives on the merits of the changes made since 1997. Labour and the Liberal Democrats believed that the programme of devolution had largely been a success. For those parties, therefore, the question was how the project might be taken forward.

Conservative	Labour	Liberal Democrats
▪ A multi-option referendum on the Welsh Assembly to include options ranging from enhanced powers through to outright abolition.	▪ Enhance the Welsh Assembly's power and work towards restoration of devolved government in Northern Ireland.	▪ More powers for devolved bodies, e.g. primary legislative powers for the Welsh Assembly.

Source: adapted from *Monitor*, the bulletin of University College London's Constitution Unit (www.ucl.ac.uk/constitution-unit), April 2005.

Table 11.4 Manifesto promises 2005

In 2004, the Richard Commission recommended that the Welsh Assembly should be granted primary legislative powers and might also gain tax varying powers from 2011. The decision of both Labour and the Liberal Democrats to endorse the broad thrust of the commission's recommendations in their 2005

Devolved bodies for Scotland and Wales

■ Labour promised devolved bodies for Scotland and Wales in its 1997 general election manifesto.

■ Referendums in Scotland and Wales in 1997 were followed by elections for a Scottish Parliament and a Welsh Assembly in 1998.

■ The new Scottish Parliament took primary legislative control of areas such as education, agriculture and law and home affairs. The second 'yes' in the referendum gave the parliament income tax varying powers.

■ The Welsh Assembly was not given primary legislative powers but could recommend legislation to the UK Parliament and had a role in overseeing Welsh quangos. It could also implement Westminster legislation in Wales. The assembly did not have the income tax varying powers afforded the Scottish Parliament.

manifestos reflected their positive experience of exercising primary legislative powers in Scotland, where the Labour–Liberal Democrat coalitions had moved to establish free long-term nursing care for the elderly, abolish top-up fees, and introduce a more effective Freedom of Information Act.

The Conservatives' more cautious approach to extending devolved powers in Wales could similarly be seen as a reaction to the way in which many aspects of government in Scotland had been placed in the hands of a body they were unlikely to control in the foreseeable future. Conservative concerns may also have been rooted in questions of legitimacy resulting from the narrow margin by which the Welsh Assembly had been established in the 1997 referendum, and the extent to which the knock-on effects of transferring primary legislative powers to the Scottish Parliament (such as the West Lothian Question) had yet to be properly addressed. The West Lothian Question may have prompted the party's 2005 commitment to 'English votes for English laws'.

Will these proposals be implemented in the short to medium term?

With both Labour and the Liberal Democrats committed to at least a partial adoption of the Richard Commission's proposals, it would appear likely that the next 5 years will see progress in this area. However, the 2005 White Paper stopped short of accepting the proposal that the Welsh Assembly should be elected under a single transferable vote system.

Regional and local government

What prompted the 2005 manifesto promises?

Under Labour there had been a proliferation of regional development bodies and other unelected local quangos between 1997 and 2005. For the Conservatives, such bodies represent an unnecessary additional level of bureaucracy. For the Liberal Democrats, the control that such bodies have over the delivery of public services raises serious questions of legitimacy and accountability. For these reasons, both parties proposed returning the powers exercised by such quangos to elected local authorities in their 2005 manifestos. Labour made no such commitment, although it did offer greater freedom for councils that performed well.

Conservative	Labour	Liberal Democrats
▪ Abolition of regional chambers and devolution of powers down to local government. ▪ Learning and Skills Councils and Strategic Health Authorities also abolished.	▪ Enhance powers of regional bodies and review powers of Greater London Authority and London mayor. ▪ More freedom for well-performing councils. ▪ The possibility of whole-council elections every 4 years.	▪ Streamlining of regional bodies and enhanced role for elected councillors rather than government appointees. ▪ More power returned from central to local government.

Source: adapted from *Monitor*, the bulletin of University College London's Constitution Unit (**www.ucl.ac.uk/constitution-unit**), April 2005.

Table 11.5 Manifesto promises 2005

The context of local government reform

- The Thatcher years saw an attack on the independence of local government, particularly in the areas of local government finance and expenditure.

- In 1997 Labour offered the prospect of a more cooperative approach that might see local authorities regain a greater degree of independence in their delivery of certain key public services.

- Since 1997, Labour has allowed local initiatives to shape authorities in line with local needs. This move has, for example, seen the emergence of US-style directly elected mayors in some areas outside of London, such as Hartlepool.

- The London-only referendum of May 1998 saw voters approve proposals for a new mayor and a strategic authority for London.

- Although the new London mayor and Greater London Assembly were not given the tax varying powers afforded to the Scottish Parliament, they took control over areas including transport and strategic planning.

- Ken Livingstone was returned as the first new mayor in the elections of 2000 and was returned for a second term in 2004.

Will these proposals be implemented in the short to medium term?
For some commentators, Labour's 2005 promise to grant top-performing local authorities more freedom of movement and the party's ongoing efforts to extend the number and power of regional bodies suggested that the plan for elected regional assemblies — apparently dead following the failure of the

November 2004 referendum in the northeast — might be revived. However, the party's 2005 manifesto made no mention of this. Such a proposal would certainly find support among Liberal Democrats, who would rather see power in the hands of elected regional assemblies than with government-appointed bureaucrats in regional agencies.

Electoral systems

What prompted the 2005 manifesto promises?

The 2005 manifestos appeared to offer little prospect of a change in the system under which general elections operate: the Conservatives said nothing; Labour merely offered a review of the systems adopted in various elections since 1997, just as they had done in 2001 (see the box below); and the Liberal Democrats stuck with their long-held support for the single transferable vote.

Conservative	Labour	Liberal Democrats
	■ Review of new electoral systems and a referendum before any change to the system used in general elections. ■ Ongoing review of how parties are operated and funded.	■ STV for general elections, local elections and devolved institutions. ■ Review of system for European Parliament elections. ■ Voting age down to 16.

Source: adapted from *Monitor*, the bulletin of University College London's Constitution Unit (www.ucl.ac.uk/constitution-unit), April 2005.

Table 11.6 Manifesto promises 2005

Spot the difference: Labour on electoral reform, 2001–05

Labour's 2001 manifesto
'We will review the experience of the new systems and the Jenkins report to assess whether changes might be made to the electoral system for the House of Commons. A referendum remains the right way to agree any change for Westminster.'

Labour's 2005 manifesto
'Labour remains committed to reviewing the experience of the new electoral systems — introduced for the devolved administrations, the European Parliament and the London Assembly. A referendum remains the right way to agree any change for Westminster.'

Although the Political Parties, Elections and Referendums Act (PPER, 2000) had required national parties to declare publicly all donations over £5,000 (see the box below), there is little to suggest that this requirement had stemmed the flow of money into the campaign coffers of the major parties, with Labour, the Conservatives and the Liberal Democrats declaring £9 million, £8 million and £4 million of donations respectively in the 2005 general election.

Parties and elections

- Allegations of sleaze and impropriety dogged the final years of John Major's administration.

- Labour's vehement criticism of such behaviour had put the party in a position where a manifesto commitment to legislate in this area was inevitable in 1997.

- The Political Parties, Elections and Referendums Act (PPER) of 2000 introduced regulation of party fundraising and spending in general election campaigns.

The PPER Act (2000)

The act sought to make parties less reliant on wealthy individual backers, challenging the perception that politics was 'for sale'. It:

- Limited party spending in general election campaigns to £30,000 per constituency.

- Required national parties to declare publicly all donations over £5,000.

Will these proposals be implemented in the short to medium term?

The paradox with electoral reform, as ever, is that a party elected with a Commons majority under first-past-the-post will inevitably be loath to change the system. Labour is no exception. The party's rejection of the Jenkins Commission's preferred AV+ system may well have reflected the fact that, if AV+ had been operating in 1997, Labour's majority of 179 would have been reduced to nearer 60. The party's relatively poor performance under the new systems adopted in other elections since 1997 (such as the devolved assembly elections, the mayoral elections in London and the European Parliament elections) may also have made Labour reluctant to move to a new system for general elections.

Citizens' rights, 1997–2005

Groups such as Charter 88 have long coveted a codified constitutional settlement that would include a fully entrenched US-style 'bill of rights'. Between 1997 and 2005 Labour had gone some way down this road.

Human Rights Act (HRA, 1998)

- This act came into force in October 2000.

- It incorporated the European Convention on Human Rights into UK law.

Freedom of Information Act (FOI, 2000)

- This act came into force in January 2005.

- It limited bureaucratic secrecy and gave citizens access to the sort of information with which they could hold governments accountable.

However, both measures have fallen some way short of what groups such as Charter 88 would have hoped for, both in their scope and in their impact.

In response to criticisms of the system in the wake of Labour being returned to office with the support of a record low of only 21.6% of the electorate, Lord Falconer said that he was not 'sure there is widespread discontent with the way the electoral system works. It has worked for some time', he noted, 'and I am not sure there is pressure for change.'

As with electoral reform, radical changes in the rules governing party finance are also unlikely. Although some argued that a move towards state funding of political parties might be necessary to restore faith in the representative model of democracy in the wake of the 2005 campaign, there appears to be little enthusiasm for such a move either with political parties or among the broader public.

Conclusion

While many would argue that further constitutional reform is at the very least desirable, it appears unlikely that major new changes will follow in the next 2 years.

Ironically, it is in an area largely avoided by the main parties in the 2005 campaign — judiciary and rights — that change is inevitable. By 2000 Labour had delivered on its 1997 manifesto commitment to provide for 'freedom of information and guaranteed human rights', to mixed reaction. The Constitutional Reform Act, which received royal assent on 24 March 2005, will extend reform into the area of judicial institutions, with the creation of a UK Supreme Court, the radical remodelling of the role of Lord Chancellor and the establishment of a new independent judicial appointments commission. These changes, hinted at in Labour's 2001 manifesto and first set out in full in 2003, are dealt with in the next chapter.

Summary

- After 18 years in opposition, Labour came into office in 1997 with a clear commitment to wide-ranging constitutional reform.
- The party had delivered on many of its 1997 manifesto commitments by 2005, although critics argued that the changes were incomplete or watered down.
- Frustration at Labour's changes led the two opposition parties to propose significant constitutional reforms in their 2005 manifestos.
- Whereas the Liberal Democrats felt that the government had not gone far enough in a range of areas, the Conservative manifesto implied that some of the changes, such as the Human Rights Act and the establishment of a Welsh Assembly, had failed.
- Prospects for significant new constitutional change in the short to medium term look fairly bleak. Expect tinkering and fine-tuning rather than further constitutional revolution.
- Changes are guaranteed in the area of judicial reform as a result of the Constitutional Reform Act (2005), passed before the general election.

Chapter 12

A new rights culture and a more independent judiciary for the UK?

About this chapter

The Human Rights Act (1998), the Freedom of Information Act (2000) and the Constitutional Reform Act (2005) have, according to some commentators, created a new 'rights culture' in the UK, while at the same time promising a judiciary that is more active in the political sphere. This chapter looks at changes in this area and, answers the following key questions:

■ What prompted Labour's decision to introduce the HRA in 1998?

■ Are the rights of UK citizens better protected now than they were in 1997?

■ What did the FOI (2000) set out to do and has it made a real difference?

■ What reforms did Labour propose for the judiciary and how many of these proposals were included in the Constitutional Reform Act (2005)?

Why did the Labour government move to offer greater protection of rights after 1997?

Commentators have traditionally drawn a distinction between 'positive' and 'negative' rights (see the box below). In the USA, the first ten amendments to the constitution, collectively known as the Bill of Rights, explicitly entrench a range of individual freedoms. Although the rights of US citizens are not, of course, confined to these clauses (a fact recognised by the 9th Amendment), the Bill of Rights has been crucial in enabling individual citizens to resist overmighty government. Similarly, the US Freedom of Information Act (1966) and the Electronic Freedom of Information Amendment (1996) have given citizens access to the information that they need to exercise their rights fully. These are examples of positive rights.

'Positive' and 'negative' rights

Positive rights are those explicitly assigned to citizens. They are often entrenched as part of the overall constitutional settlement.

Negative rights are those that are not explicitly set out, but which exist in the absence of any law forbidding individuals from exercising them.

In contrast, up to 1997 the UK was said to have a culture of negative rights. This absence of a clear and concise summary of the rights available to UK citizens prompted Labour to take on board the ideas of groups such as Charter

88 and bring two key pieces of rights legislation — the Human Rights Act (HRA) in 1998 and the Freedom of Information Act (FOI) in 2000 — onto the statute books during its first term in government. These developments have led some to suggest that the UK is developing a new positive rights culture.

Rights in Britain pre-1997

- The UK had neither a codified constitution nor a US-style bill of rights.
- Instead the UK constitution and the statutory framework evolved over time, with citizens remaining free to do anything that had not been legislated against.
- Those individual rights that had been established under common law or statute were vulnerable to statutory limitations.
- There was no right to government-held information or data. Government operated within a culture of secrecy.
- The UK was, therefore, said to have a culture of 'negative rights'.

What is the Human Rights Act?

- The HRA (1998) came into force in October 2000.
- It incorporates most of the articles of the 1950 European Convention on Human Rights (ECHR) into UK law.
- It includes: the right to life (article 2), the right to a fair trial (article 6), the right to family and private life (article 8), and freedom of expression (article 10).
- As the HRA is based upon the Council of Europe's ECHR, rather than on EU law, it is not superior to parliamentary statute (which EU laws are, under the Treaty of Rome).
- Despite this, the HRA (like the ECHR) has a persuasive authority that has enhanced the protection of individual rights in the UK.

Does the HRA mean that the rights of UK citizens are better protected now than they were in 1997?

The HRA was never likely to live up to the billing given to it by its instigator, the then home secretary Jack Straw.

First, the HRA is neither entrenched nor superior to regular parliamentary statute. Courts cannot, therefore, use the HRA to strike down acts of parliament — they may merely issue a declaration of incompatibility, thereby inviting parliament to reconsider the offending statute. Similarly, key sections of the HRA can be derogated (or suspected) when the government feels that circumstances necessitate such a move, as happened following the attacks on the USA on 11 September 2001 and the UK on 7 July 2005.

The HRA: an assessment

'When Jack Straw, then home secretary, incorporated the European Convention on Human Rights into UK law under the HRA, he claimed that the nation would acquire something like the USA's Bill of Rights.

In contrast, the 5 years since the HRA came into force have seen tabloid newspapers reporting that the Human Rights Act has brought nothing but chaos, with asylum seekers, gypsies and prisoners harnessing innocent-seeming rights to liberty and family life in such a way as to trample on everyone else's liberties.

In reality, the incorporation of the ECHR into domestic law has not come close to meeting the reformers' hopes — nor has it confirmed the conservatives' fears.'

Source: adapted from 'The menace that wasn't', *The Economist*, 11 November 2004.

Second, it was unrealistic to think that UK rights culture would be transformed overnight simply by the passing of such a measure. It will clearly take time for the rights protected by the HRA to enter the public consciousness and longer still before significant numbers of ordinary citizens are moved to employ these rights in legal action. Early cases saw the act being used by celebrities such as Naomi Campbell, Michael Douglas and Catherine Zeta Jones, and Zoë Ball to protect their privacy, rather than by the 'ordinary citizens' whom Jack Straw intended the HRA to benefit. However, recent years have seen more widespread and ground-breaking use of the act, such as to appeal against the detention of terrorist suspects.

The HRA and the detention of terrorist suspects

A (FC) and others (FC) (Appellants) v *Secretary of State for the Home Department* (Respondent)

On 16 December 2004, an appellate committee of nine Law Lords ruled (8:1) that the indefinite detention of suspects under the Anti-terrorism, Crime and Security Act (2001) was incompatible with the European Convention on Human Rights, as incorporated into UK law in the Human Rights Act (1998):

'We consider the shortcomings described above to be sufficiently serious to strongly recommend that the Part 4 powers which allow foreign nationals to be detained potentially indefinitely should be replaced as a matter of urgency. New legislation should:

(a) deal with terrorism, whatever its origin or the nationality of its suspected perpetrators; and

(b) not require a derogation from the European Convention on Human Rights.'

This prompted home secretary Charles Clarke to draft new anti-terrorist measures.

Third, the public impact of the HRA has been limited by the fact that draft legislation is now examined by parliament's Joint Committee on Human Rights to ensure that it will not be incompatible with the rights already incorporated.

This means that, although the number of HRA cases arising from new legislation should be relatively few, the act is still having a significant, if less visible, impact on the way in which law is made.

What did the FOI seek to do and has it made a real difference?

The Freedom of Information Act (FOI)

The FOI received royal assent on 30 November 2000, but did not come into force until 1 January 2005. This delay in implementation was supposed to provide public authorities with an opportunity to prepare for the anticipated avalanche of requests for information.

What did the FOI do?
- It gave citizens the right to access information held by public authorities.
- It required public bodies seeking to deny requests for information to show that the public interest warrants an exemption under the act.
- It established a new Information Commissioner and Information Tribunal.
- It required public authorities to adopt a scheme for the publication of information.

In much the same way as the HRA initially failed to live up to its billing, the FOI did not lead to the avalanche of requests for information that had been anticipated (see the box below). Public authorities, ranging from government departments to local police and fire authorities, had spent 5 years preparing for 'information D-day' on 1 January 2005. In many cases, additional staff had been taken on specifically to deal with requests from the public. In reality, however, the initial uptake was relatively small.

Anticipating the FOI

'Potentially the most explosive section of the new act will be its retrospective provisions. Police Authorities are gearing up to pre-empt what could be a flood of requests. There is likely to be a rash of demands for information on the Hillsborough tragedy, the Toxteth and Brixton riots, the miners' dispute and the poll tax riots in London. In Northern Ireland, which is committed to introducing the act at the same time as England and Wales...it is predicted that there will be a "tidal wave" of requests.'

Mark Lobel, 'Freedom of Information Act guide', *Guardian*, 15 July 2003.

Most early requests for information came not from individual citizens but from media organisations, which saw the act either as a means of tying up loose ends on earlier stories or as a new tool of investigative journalism. For example, the *Guardian* used the act to run a range of articles between July and September 2005. Other newspapers used the information available under the act to squeeze extra mileage out of old stories, such as the arrest of Rolling Stones front man Mick Jagger in 1969.

The FOI and the *Guardian*

Operation of the Common Agricultural Policy (CAP) (published 24 July 2005)
'Farmers in some of the richest parts of England [get] the lion's share of subsidies under the CAP. The policy's defenders argue that it supports small, poor farmers...but [information] released under the FOI shows that while the South East received £212m of subsidies last year, just £86m went to the North West and £96m to the North East.'

The inquiry into the death of Diana, Princess of Wales (published 11 August 2005)
'The cost of Scotland Yard's investigation into the death of the Princess of Wales...could reach £2m, based on figures released under the Freedom of Information Act. Salaries for the 14-strong team make up most of the spending.'

Local authority food inspection reports (published 14 September 2005)
'The *Guardian* submitted requests to a number of local councils for copies of reports of inspections which had been conducted since November 2004.' (The results were then published, by authority, on the *Guardian Unlimited* website.)

Source: adapted from various articles in the *Guardian*.

As happened with the HRA, however, the FOI will inevitably see more use as it enters the public consciousness. In July 2005, for example, Lord Falconer was forced to reveal details of his ministerial diary and by October 2005 *Metro* was reporting that Michael Hanney, a man short-listed for a job with a regional development agency, had used the FOI to obtain the notes made by the panel at his interview, thus enabling him to win his High Court case for sexual discrimination against health secretary Patricia Hewitt.

Why did Labour propose changes to the judiciary and how were these proposals received?

The traditional roles of the Lord Chancellor and the prime minister in the appointment of judges had led to accusations of the politicisation of the judiciary. In 2003 Labour announced plans to abolish the post of Lord Chancellor and to enhance further the separation of powers by establishing an independent Judicial Appointments Commission. Labour also proposed the creation of a US-style Supreme Court in line with the broad commitment to reform the judiciary outlined in its 2001 general election manifesto.

These proposals faced opposition, in the Lords and among senior members of the judiciary. This opposition was rooted both in the substance of the changes proposed (particularly the proposal to remove the House of Lords' judicial function) and in the manner of their announcement (particularly the attempt to abolish the 400-year-old position of Lord Chancellor through cabinet reshuffle). It was said that the then Lord Chief Justice, Lord Woolf, was only informed of the proposed changes 1 hour before the release of the plan, leading to further accusations of government by press release.

Labour and judicial reform

On 12 June 2003, the government announced proposals for far-reaching constitutional changes, in line with commitments made in the Labour Party's 2001 manifesto. These included:

- The abolition of the office of Lord Chancellor (who, among other responsibilities, is head of the judiciary, appoints judges and can sit as a member of the Appellate Committee).

- The establishment of a new UK Supreme Court separate from the House of Lords and the removal of the Law Lords from the legislature.

- A new independent Judicial Appointments Commission.

- A new Department for Constitutional Affairs to replace the Lord Chancellor's Department.

Source: House of Lords, www.parliament.uk

What does the Constitutional Reform Act actually do?

Despite widespread opposition, the Constitutional Reform Bill was introduced into the Lords on 24 February 2004 and finally received royal assent on 24 March 2005. The act included most of the measures outlined in 2003, with one or two key exceptions and refinements.

The Constitutional Reform Act (2005)

The act addresses four key areas:

- *Judicial independence.* Government ministers will be required by law to uphold the independence of the judiciary.

- *Reforming the role of the Lord Chancellor.* The judicial functions of the Lord Chancellor will be transferred to the President of the Courts of England and Wales. This post is to be held by the Lord Chief Justice.

- *Supreme Court.* There will be a new, independent Supreme Court. It will be separate from the House of Lords and will have its own staff, budget and building.

- *Judicial Appointments Commission.* There will be a new independent Judicial Appointments Commission. It will recommend candidates to the secretary of state for constitutional affairs for his confirmation.

Source: Department of Constitutional Affairs, adapted from www.dca.gov.uk

The role of Lord Chancellor will remain, although the incumbent will no longer serve both as a government minister and as a judge. This will address long-standing concerns regarding the incomplete separation, or 'fusion', of powers in the UK system of government. Specifically, it will address concerns that the presence of the Lord Chancellor in the executive, legislature and judiciary contravenes the ECHR guarantee of a fair trial.

The House of Lords will create a new position of speaker (a 'Lord' or 'Lady Speaker') and the Lord Chancellor will not take this position by right. The government roles of the Lord Chancellor will, as at present, be exercised by the secretary of state for constitutional affairs. The Department of Constitutional Affairs, shorn of its role in judicial appointments and training — which will be taken over by the new Independent Appointments Commission and the President of the Courts of England and Wales respectively — will become more akin to a US-style Justice Department.

The new UK Supreme Court will comprise the current Law Lords in the first instance, in a move that sees the upper house losing its judicial function. Subsequent appointments to the new court will be under the control of the Independent Judicial Appointments Commission. Under the act, this commission will present a single name to the secretary of state for constitutional affairs for his or her confirmation.

The fact that the Supreme Court will have its own staff, its own budget and — eventually — its own building, should send a clear message regarding the independence of a judiciary that has become significantly more assertive in its use of judicial review in recent years.

The rise of judicial review in the UK

The creation of a UK Supreme Court comes at a time when the senior members of the judiciary in the UK are already more active in the political sphere than they have ever been. Their powers of judicial review have been enhanced by two clear developments:

- Judges are increasingly being called on to adjudicate when UK statutes appear to violate EU law. Under the *Factortame* case (1990), UK courts gained the power to suspend UK statutes that appeared to be in violation of EU law until the European Court of Justice could make a final determination.

- The incorporation of the ECHR into UK law under the HRA has brought senior judges into direct conflict with government (for example, over the indefinite detention of terrorist suspects).

There are, however, a number of unknowns with respect to the Constitutional Reform Act:

- The precise composition of the Independent Appointments Commission will be crucial and this was not clearly set out in the act. How independent will the process of appointing the Independent Commission be?
- What will happen if the secretary of state for constitutional affairs refuses to accept the recommendation of the commission?
- How powerful will the new Supreme Court be in the absence of a codified constitution with entrenched rights?
- Will the creation of a UK Supreme Court bring the senior judiciary under close media scrutiny? Will the Supreme Court justices become public figures?

The last two questions are probably the hardest to answer. As has been the case with the HRA and the FOI, it is likely that the court will take time to establish itself in the public consciousness. The relationship between the court, the public, the government and parliament will also take time to formalise. In this respect, the UK Supreme Court may have more in common with its US counterpart than one would initially think. After all, the latter's power of judicial review was not set out explicitly in Article III of the constitution, but was discovered by the court itself in cases such as *Marbury* v *Madison* (1803). It may be that the new UK Supreme Court will have to carve out a role for itself in a similar way.

Conclusion

Labour's efforts to establish a new rights culture in the UK and to reform the judiciary have not met with universal approval. Those on the left have accused the party of introducing watered-down versions of the reforms proposed by groups such as Charter 88. Those on the right, in contrast, have seen the HRA and the FOI as tools all too easily deployed by minorities in defence of practices that impinge on the liberties of the majority. They fear that a Supreme Court will result in the politicisation of the judiciary and the further under-mining of parliamentary sovereignty. Whatever the truth may be, one thing is clear. The full impact of the reforms introduced since 1998 will not become apparent for a decade or more.

Summary

- Prior to 1997 the UK was seen as having a culture of negative rights.
- The HRA (1998), which incorporated the ECHR into UK law, came into force in October 2000.
- Although the ECHR and the HRA do not have the same legal authority as EU law, they have a persuasive authority in the sense that ministers seek to avoid acting in a manner that might be deemed incompatible with the HRA.
- The cases brought under the HRA may not increase in number, due to the work of parliament's Joint Committee on Human Rights. However, those cases that are brought in the future might be more significant.
- The FOI (2000) did not come into force until January 2005 and it is probably too early to assess its true impact.
- The Constitutional Reform Act (2005) enhances the separation of powers and establishes a UK Supreme Court.
- The full impact of the changes brought by the Constitutional Reform Act, the HRA and the FOI may not be apparent for a decade or more.

Greater powers for sub-national and supranational government?

About this chapter

Between 1997 and 2005 the Labour government established a number of regional bodies, some elected and some unelected. These years also saw a broadening and deepening of the European Union. This chapter focuses on the future of devolved government post-2005 as well as considering likely developments regarding the EU. In doing so it addresses key questions, such as:

- Will the power of unelected regional bodies increase or decline in the next few years?
- Is the plan for elected assemblies in the English regions really dead?
- How might the structure, scope and powers of the Welsh Assembly change?
- What impact will EU enlargement have on its institutions and everyday operation?
- How is Europe likely to move forward in the wake of the rejection of the new EU constitution?

Will the power of unelected regional bodies change?

It was widely believed that the establishment of devolved bodies in Scotland, Wales and Northern Ireland would limit the number and power of unelected quangos in those countries. Indeed, the changes resulted in the creation of the the post of commissioner for public appointments, one for Northern Ireland and one for Wales, as well as giving the Welsh Assembly oversight of the team of independent assessors that would fill positions on Welsh quangos. Despite these moves, however, quangos appear to have retained a significant role in those areas now governed by devolved bodies.

Quangos in Scotland and Wales

There were still 3,500 appointed positions on Scottish quangos and 4,500 in Wales in 2005. In Wales these bodies accounted for £1.22 billion of public spending in the financial year 2003–04.

Source: Julie Macleavy and Oonagh Gay, 'The quango debate', House of Commons Research Paper 05/30, April 2005.

Similarly, the establishment of regional development agencies in England in 1998 has seen even more control placed in the hands of unelected, and some would say unaccountable, quangocrats.

Regional quangos in England

English regional quangos, such as the regional development agencies (RDAs) established in 1998, have a major role in coordinating government policy. The Department of Trade and Industry estimates that the eight RDAs will receive a total of £2.15 billion in 2005–06, rising to £2.31 billion in 2007–08.

Concerns regarding such bodies persisted in the 2005 general election, when both Liberal Democrats and Conservatives proposed transferring quango powers and funding back into the hands of directly elected local councillors. Although Labour's general election victory makes such a move unlikely, it is conceivable that an effort to relaunch the plan for elected regional authorities or to enhance the powers of the Welsh Assembly would see the number and scope of such unelected bodies reduced significantly.

The Conservatives and the regions

'Under Mr Blair, the way we are governed has become less accountable, more complex and, ultimately, less democratic. Ministers don't take responsibility for their failures. Unprecedented powers have been given to new, unelected and remote bodies, including regional assemblies for which there is no popular support.

Conservatives understand that people identify with their town, city or county, not with arbitrary "regions". We will abolish Labour's regional assemblies. Powers currently exercised at a regional level covering planning, housing, transport and the fire service will all be returned to local authorities.'

Source: adapted from the 2005 Conservative Party manifesto.

Is the plan for elected assemblies in the English regions really dead?

Labour went into the 2001 general election with a commitment to extending the process of devolution to the English regions. By November 2004, however, this programme had stalled, with voters in the northeast rejecting the opportunity to have their own elected regional assembly. The deputy prime minister later announced that the referendums planned for other regions, but suspended pending the outcome of the poll in the northeast, would not go ahead.

The northeast referendum

'On 4th November [2004], a proposal to establish an elected regional assembly was turned down by voters in the North East in a referendum on regional government. Turnout for the referendum was almost 48% with 22% voting in favour and 78% voting against the proposal.

On 8th November, the Deputy Prime Minister made a statement to Parliament on the North East result. The Deputy Prime Minister also confirmed that postponed referendums in the North West and Yorkshire and the Humber would now not take place.

However, the Government continues to have a clear policy to decentralise power and improve performance through reform in local government and strengthening all the English regions.'

Source: Office of the Deputy Prime Minister's website, www.odpm.gov.uk.

Although Labour went into the 2005 general election offering to devolve even greater powers to the regions (see the box below), it was not committed to turning regional government into locally elected and accountable regional assemblies. The consequence of this, of course, is that the existing unelected regional development agencies and other bodies will gain greater power as opposed to seeing their powers transferred to locally elected bodies.

The 2005 Labour Party manifesto and regional government

'In our first term, we devolved power to Scotland and Wales and restored city-wide government to London. Britain is stronger as a result. In the next Parliament, we will decentralise power further. In Wales we will develop democratic devolution by creating a stronger Assembly with enhanced legislative powers and a reformed structure and electoral system to make the exercise of Assembly responsibilities clearer and more accountable to the public. We will also review the powers of the London Mayor and the Greater London Authority. And we will devolve further responsibility to existing regional bodies in relation to planning, housing, economic development and transport.'

Source: Labour Party manifesto, 2005.

How might the structure, scope and powers of the Welsh Assembly change?

In June 2005, the government published its White Paper on reforming the form, function, and efficiency of the Welsh Assembly. This paper, entitled

Recommendations of the Richard Commission (2004)

- Wales should have its own legislative assembly with primary legislative powers.
- Tax-varying powers on the Scottish model would be desirable, but not essential.
- The devolution of such additional powers will necessitate an increase in the assembly's membership from 60 to 80.
- STV provides a more appropriate way in which to elect this larger assembly than the current AMS system.
- The new assembly should be reconstituted as a separate legislature and executive.

Source: conclusions of the summary report of the Richard Commission.

'Better Governance for Wales', provided a more formal response to the recommendations made by the Richard Commission (see the box above).

'Better Governance for Wales' offered the prospect of an enhanced assembly, but stopped some way short of adopting Lord Richard's recommendations in full.

'Better Governance for Wales' (2005)

This White Paper set out government proposals to change the provisions of the Government of Wales Act (1998) in three key respects.

To create a new executive structure for the assembly
Under the Government of Wales Act (1998) there was no formal separation between the assembly and the Welsh Assembly government. The White Paper proposed further legislation to create a distinct Welsh executive.

To give the assembly enhanced legislative powers
The White Paper noted that of the 23 bids for primary legislation made by the assembly between 1998 and 2005, 17 had resulted in legislation or legislative proposals. Despite this, the government proposed giving the assembly 'enhanced legislative powers in defined policy areas where it already has executive functions', although this would fall short of the primary legislative powers envisaged by the Richard Commission. The White Paper confirmed that the granting of primary legislative powers would come only in the long term, and would even then be subject to public approval through a further Welsh referendum.

To deal with some of the problems associated with the AMS electoral system currently in place
Having modified Lord Richard's proposals for changes to the composition and powers of the assembly, the White Paper also rejected the commission's call for the adoption of the STV system in assembly elections. Instead the government offered reform of the current AMS system so as to prevent candidates standing both in constituency elections and on the party lists employed in the top-up.

Source: 'Better Governance for Wales' (The Stationery Office, June 2005).

It was hoped that a more formal separation between an executive and the assembly might make the devolved institutions more accessible to the Welsh public. The system set up under the Government of Wales Act (1998) had, it was argued, resulted in a lack of clarity regarding who exactly did what within the devolved authority. The arrangements proposed in the White Paper would see the creation of a formal executive (or cabinet) which had clear responsibilities and would be accountable to the assembly, with the assembly in turn being accountable to voters. The result would be a new Welsh Assembly government.

The first minister would be nominated from among Assembly Members (AMs) by the assembly, before being formally appointed by the monarch. He or she would then have the power to appoint other ministers with the monarch's approval. Civil servants, who had previously been torn between serving the assembly and those AMs who were delegated powers as ministers, would be able to act exclusively on behalf of the Welsh Assembly government under the new arrangements.

The enhanced legislative powers proposed under the White Paper, though falling short of the primary legislative powers suggested by Lord Richard, would mark a significant extension of the assembly's effective powers. As the White Paper stated, 'the Government believes that it is now time to re-balance legislative authority towards the Assembly, without affecting the overall constitutional supremacy of Parliament as regards Wales within the United Kingdom'. One aspect of this enhanced legislative role would involve greater participation by the assembly at the drafting stage. Another proposal would see the assembly given the power to 'amend, repeal, or extend the provisions of Acts of Parliament in their application to Wales'.

The decision to prevent candidates from standing simultaneously in both constituency elections and list elections resulted from the way in which the AMS system used in Welsh Assembly elections had been abused in 1999 and 2003. In Clwyd West in 2003, the White Paper noted, four of the five candidates who stood for the single-member assembly constituency eventually ended up as Assembly Members — one by winning the constituency race under FPTP, and another three elected from their party's lists under the top-up procedure. The government argued that this abuse of the AMS system ran the risk of acting as 'a disincentive to vote in constituency elections'.

What impact will EU enlargement have on its institutions and everyday operation?

The Treaty of Nice (2001) addressed the theme of EU enlargement and the reorganisation of EU institutions that this would necessitate. In particular, the treaty dealt with the way in which qualified majority voting (QMV) would have to be extended into far more areas, because proceeding on the basis of unanimity would be impossible once the number of states in the EU exceeded 20.

The Treaty of Nice (2001)

The treaty:

- Provided for the extension of the European Parliament's co-decision powers into new areas and allowed the reapportioning of parliament seats between member states.

- Brought a restructuring of the European Commission, with one commissioner for each of the 25 member states from January 2005.

- Extended the use of QMV into new areas and provided for the reapportionment of votes between the states in an enlarged Union.

In effect, the extension of QMV, and the reapportionment of votes between member states, means that countries will have to engage in coalition building with their allies in order to achieve the number of votes required to block or pass a measure under QMV.

Turkey was not among the 15 states admitted to the EU in January 2005. However, it was announced on 3 October that formal negotiations regarding the accession of what would be the Union's first majority Muslim state were imminent. These negotiations are likely to take up to 15 years, so several other nations are set to join before Turkey. The European Union (Accessions) Bill introduced into the House of Commons on 11 October 2005, for example, sought to provide UK approval for the Treaty of Accession signed in Luxembourg in April 2005. Under this treaty, Bulgaria and Romania will join the EU from January 2007, provided the European Commission is satisfied that they have met the various entry requirements.

It is inevitable that not only the institutions, but also the character of the EU, will be affected by the ongoing programme of enlargement. A Union of 27 or more sovereign states is obviously going to behave rather differently from the much smaller club of nine states that the UK joined in 1973. This, in part, explains the EU's decision to try and codify a formal constitution at the end of 2004.

How is Europe likely to move forward in the wake of the rejection of the new EU constitution?

The enlargement of the EU from 15 to 25 member states in January 2005 marked a significant watershed at the end of an extended period of change in the Union. Starting with measures such as the Single European Act (1986) and including the Maastricht Treaty (1992), the EU had changed out of all recognition from the EEC founded in the 1950s. For the governments of many member states, therefore, 2005 marked a suitable point at which to codify the various treaties that constituted the EU into a single authoritative constitution.

A new constitution for the EU?

The proposed constitution ran to over 400 pages. It sought to bring together the various existing treaties into a single codified document that set out the rules of the EU.

The proposed constitution did not grant the EU any additional powers. Instead, it would have:

- strengthened the role of the European Parliament
- enhanced the role of national parliaments in revising EU law
- extended QMV into 26 policy areas that previously allowed the national veto, such as asylum

It was this new constitution, formally signed by the heads of member states on 29 October 2004, that was up for ratification in a series of national referendums, starting with the French on 29 May 2005. The French rejection of the constitution, and the Dutch rejection that followed on 1 June, again by referendum, constituted a genuine crisis for the EU. Opinions differed as to why French and Dutch voters had moved in such numbers (55% in France, 62% in the Netherlands) against the ratification of the new constitution. For some, the public opposition was a result of fears regarding the supposed rise of a 'United States of Europe'. For others, it was a result of the economic fallout from the adoption of the euro.

Why the rejections?

The following reasons have been suggested for the rejection of the EU constitution in France and the Netherlands:

- erosion of national sovereignty and national identity
- general uneasiness with the EU
- the amount and increasing scope of legislation from Brussels
- Turkish accession to the EU
- Anglo-Saxon economic liberalism reducing the focus on 'social Europe'
- globalisation
- loss of national influence in Europe
- EU integration going too fast
- EU influence over issues close to citizens
- lack of democracy in the EU
- the euro

Source: Vaughne Miller, 'The future of the European Union', House of Commons Research Paper 05/45, June 2005.

Although some member states did approve the treaty in the wake of the French and Dutch votes, the requirement that the constitution be ratified by all 25 member states meant that the measure was effectively dead. The UK government's decision to suspend the passage of the European Union Bill — which would have approved the constitution subject to a UK-wide referendum — merely bowed to the inevitable.

Where to from here?

A number of options present themselves:

(1) Revive the constitution and submit it to fresh referendums in those countries where it was rejected.

(2) Redraft the constitution so as to address the concerns that provoked opposition.

(3) Abandon plans for a new constitution and persist with existing arrangements.

(4) Proceed with those aspects of the new constitution that do not require formal ratification, and leave the more thorny questions until a later date.

There is some precedent for option 1. When the Irish rejected the Treaty of Nice by referendum on 7 June 2001, for example, their government brought forward a second referendum, campaigned more effectively and secured a clear 'yes' vote on 19 October 2002. The situation in 2005 is, however, somewhat different from that in 2001. Opposition to the constitution is far more widespread and deep-rooted than it was in 2001. Moreover, the consequences of a second defeat at the hands of voters would be unthinkable.

Option 2 clearly has some merit. The treaty could be renegotiated in such a way as to place some of its more controversial elements into protocols that member states could opt out of — as occurred with the Social Chapter and economic and monetary union in the Maastricht Treaty (1992). We should remember, however, that the constitution rejected by French voters was itself the product of long and painful negotiations as well as a good deal of brinkmanship on all sides. Is there any real possibility that further negotiations would result in a proposal that was any more acceptable to the voters in one or more member states? Wouldn't it just result in a two-track EU, rather than providing the simple, codified 'rulebook-for-all' that the constitution was supposed to be?

Option 3 is more of a default position than a realistic option in itself. In the absence of a new constitution, the EU would, of course, continue to operate under the existing treaties, as amended by the Treaty of Nice (2001). The expansion of the Union from 2005 has, however, created a situation in which the drafting of a more concise, codified set of rules is clearly necessary — a point often lost amid the tabloid frenzy regarding mass immigration and asylum.

Option 4 was the pragmatic approach supported by many commentators in the wake of the French and Dutch votes. Not all elements of the constitution agreed in 2004 require formal amendment of the current treaties (see the box below). The EU could, therefore, move ahead in some areas while leaving

Moving ahead without a new constitution

'Elements of the constitution and some reforms linked to it could be implemented without Treaty amendment, either because their legal basis is provided by existing Treaty articles, or because they can be implemented by intergovernmental or inter-institutional agreements. These might include institutional reforms that address the "democratic deficit" and other, more innovative, elements, such as the proposed EU diplomatic service, the EU defence agency, the rapid reaction forces, the European gendarmerie and the Fundamental Rights Agency.'

Source: Vaughne Miller, 'The future of the European Union', House of Commons Research Paper 05/45, June 2005.

others to one side. This so-called 'Nice Plus' approach would result in the broadening of the enhanced cooperation agreed under the Treaty of Nice, but would stop short of providing a single codified constitution in place of the existing treaties.

What was the state of play in November 2005?

By the middle of June 2005, Jean-Claude Juncker, prime minister of Luxembourg (then holder of the EU presidency), acknowledged that while the timetable for introducing the new EU constitution was clearly dead, a new schedule would not be considered until mid-2006 at the earliest. This took the pressure off those countries — not least the UK — that had yet to hold their own referendums.

By 21 September 2005, the President of the Commission, José Manuel Barroso, was conceding that the delay would be longer still. 'In all probability,' he acknowledged, 'at least for the next 2 or 3 years, we will not have a constitution.' In the meantime, he argued, the EU should not be paralysed but should focus on '[getting] things done that ordinary people can see and appreciate. We should not focus our efforts exclusively on devising institutional scenarios' (*Guardian*, 22 September 2005).

By the time of the summit of EU leaders held at Hampton Court in late October under the UK presidency, the *Guardian* was able to publish an article of over 600 words without a single reference to the future of the constitution. Instead it focused on Blair's five-point plan, which comprised:
- a common EU energy policy
- a coordination of reform of European universities
- increased spending on research and development
- controlling migration flows
- improving work–life balance

Although the EU constitution agreed in 2004 is clearly dead, the Union moves on. It is interesting to note that Blair's agenda carefully skirted around the thorny issues of further reform of the Common Agricultural Policy and the UK's longstanding budget rebate.

Conclusion

Labour's victory in the 2005 general election appeared to offer the prospect of a significant change in the relationship between regional, national and European government. In reality, however, such change was always unlikely, and became increasingly so over the course of 2005. The failure to secure an elected assembly for the northeast in the referendum of November 2004 meant that the future of regional government was likely to lie in the direction of a further enhancement of unelected regional agencies. Similarly, as regards the Welsh Assembly, Labour's election manifesto and the 'Better Governance for Wales' White Paper that followed the election made it clear that the party did

not intend to implement fully the recommendations of the Richard Commission (2004). Finally, in respect of Europe, the failure to adopt the new constitution, a document that Labour had long argued was merely a tidying-up exercise, meant that the Union was forced to move forward in a more pragmatic and piecemeal fashion.

Summary

- The Labour Party put a good deal of power into the hands of unelected regional bodies between 1997 and 2005. It is likely that these bodies will be enhanced further in the coming months.

- The Welsh Assembly is set to become a more influential body, but it will not gain all of the powers envisaged by the Richard Commission.

- The ongoing enlargement of the European Union will necessitate further structural changes and will also affect the Union's character.

- The rejection of the EU constitution has not proved quite as catastrophic as some commentators predicted.